Wolfpak
Sh*t You Don't Get Merit Badges For
© Mark Drake 2020
All rights reserved

Illustrations by Mark Drake © 2020

ISBN 9798585749070

Published by Wolfpak LLC
11426 Davis St. #551.
Grand Blanc, MI 48480
www.wolfpak.live

Without limiting the rights under copyright reserved above, no part of this publication may be reproduced, stored in or introduced into a retrieval system, transmitted, in any form or by any means (electronic, mechanical, photocopying, recording, or otherwise), without the prior written permission of the copyright owner.

GRATITUDE

To the Lord, our Father, thank you. I never understood the whole "Father," bit until I was a grown man. Yet, here I am. I never understood the complexity of how we are "All God's children." Yet, here I am. It has been an incredible journey of momentous highs, and grave lows, to get to this point. Yet, here I am… and I see now- that you were always by my side.

I didn't know you, and you loved me. I found you, and you loved me. I pushed you away, and you loved me. I straight up hated you, and you loved me. I fell down, and you loved me. I gave up, and you loved me. I failed you, and you loved me.

Even though I thought that I was alone, I know you were there. When I was crawling through the darkness, it was you who guided me. When I was ready to give up, it was you who continued to push me to keep going. Just like a Father, who loves his son.

You let me venture off when I thought I knew everything, and accepted me when I found out that I was wrong. You looked over me as I endured the bumps and bruises of life, and picked me up when I couldn't get up on my own. You let me seek answers, even though they would only lead me back to you. Just like a Father, who loves his son.

You have been there when I called out in desperation, and offered your love and grace even though I was unworthy of any of it… Just like a Father, who loves his son.

Thank you, Lord, for loving me in spite of my childlike ignorance, stupidity, tantrums, and mistakes. Thank you for loving me when I took it for granted, ignored it, and even rejected it.

I know the language in this book isn't appropriate for any church. However, I hope you understand; I am trying to free people from the burdens they carry which prevent them from reaching their full potential. It is my hope that this book achieves that by helping people find, and truly feel, the happiness you have shown me.

Thank you, Lord, for blessing me with your grace- and being with me on this incredible journey through life.

Amen.

2 Corinthians 12:9
My grace is sufficient for you, for power is made perfect in weakness

To my wife- thank you for your continuous love and support as we surf the waves of life together- forever. Even though there were difficult waves for us both, I'm grateful that we learned how to ride them together. I have realized that you give me balance- and without balance, it's hard to walk, much less, ride a wave that is crushing downward. Thank you for the love you share. I look forward to the future ahead of us. Know that I love you.

To my daughter- I love you. It is my hope that this book gives you a better understanding of who your father is, and moreover, that it will allow me to pass my knowledge onto you if my time to depart this world comes before you are in need of it. You have been the light of my life, know that I love you forever and always.

To my mother- thank you for giving me kindness, caring, and continuous love and support. Thank you for showing me that where you come from doesn't determine who you are, or determine where you end, as we all have to the power to choose who we want to be. Know that I love you.

To my father- thank you for giving me strength and determination to weather any storm I encountered. Thank you for showing me the power of determination, regardless of what the world says otherwise. Know that I love you.

To my brother- thank you for keeping me humble, and always being my friend. Know that I love you.

To my angel in heaven- thank you for watching over me as I crawled through the darkness. Thank you for teaching me how to find happiness. Know that I love and miss you, but you're always in my heart.

To my friends over the years (in alphabetical order): 'G' Abrol, Aparna (Echempati) Bankston, Andrew Barbour, Ben Beckley, C. Drew Bethka, Norman Burge, Andy Bush, Dave Capriccioso, Katrina Coleman, Brent Corbin, Aaron Culloty, Kyle Darling, Dennis A. Donald 'DAD', Leslie Ely, Tony Ford, Jon Fortin, Andy Gadd, Jason Garrick, Chad Gillies, Kevin Goodcourage, Brad Griffus, Erin (Kennedy) Hamlin, Bethany Harris, Dennis Hartman, Chelsea (Clark) Hawley, John Hill, Jeff Helias, Chris Horne, Andy and Krystle Howell, Bob Hoyer, Isaac Ireland, Nick Jannakos, Tracy Jay, Jeremy Jones, Natalie Karpac, Gary and Mary Keefer, Chris 'Ripcord' Kososki, John Knopp, John Lazarski, Alex Lucido, Ashley McMurray, Cindy Miraz, Kevin Moczul, James Muhleck, Eric Naber, Scott Nielson, Don Noble, Lia (Bottinelli) O'Toole, Demetrius 'Meach' Owens, Tim Peasel, Joe Perry, Tylene Porter, Matt Racine, Peter Rahn, Chris and Jessica Rodrigues, Tom Ruffley, Jeff Sano, Jim Skarl, Jeff Smith, Dave Stohl, William 'Azim' Sulton, Ryan Thick, Tracy Till, Kathy Tobe, Lance Truax, Matt Truax, Geoff Ward, Carmen Williams, Derek Williams, and Joslyn Wilkerson: thank you all for the memories that we have shared*.

* If you expected your name to appear, but didn't see it, please know that you haven't been forgotten in my heart (I probably just didn't remember your last name). I am grateful that you were a part of my life.

TABLE OF CONTENTS

Introduction

Forward: The "Secrets" that sell millions of books

Learned Hopelessness

Behavior

Happiness

Fear

Addiction

Depression

Gratitude

Relationships

Achieving Success

Leadership

INTRODUCTION

Some people are going to be offended by this book. If you are one of those people, I'm sorry, and ask that you give this book back to the person who gave it to you, or put it back on the shelf (even the wrong shelf next to some super-popular book is ok) because this book isn't meant for you.

If you are looking for a book written by some doctor (M.D./Ph.D.) who is going to drone on about their own personal bullshit for 150 pages and then try to sell you some incredible new technique that she/he "discovered," (which is nothing but 'The Power of Positive Thinking' rebooted... again) for another 150 pages this book isn't for you. There is no instant cure- if you expected one, that's part of the problem you have.

If you are looking for someone to bullshit you and tell you that it's the world's fault that you're all fucked up- this book isn't for you. I'm sorry, but you have to take accountability for your own shit too.

So, who is this book for? This book is for someone who doesn't like to read books. It's for people who wouldn't be caught dead with a "Self-help," book. This book is for someone who knows that their life sucks, and is truly ready to do whatever it takes to make it better. This book is for someone who is looking for information from a real person and not some arrogant asshole who uses "doctor talk," to sound more intelligent than what he/she really is.

The problem with Ph.D.'s (doctors) is that many went straight from their bachelor's degree, to master's degree, then to their Ph.D., and then formed all of their "professional," opinions based on what they were directly taught.

Other doctors base their opinions on surveys (as the basis of "research") which were given to college kids on the campus where they completed their dissertation (big research paper to get their "Doctorate" degree).

Those "experts," fail to understand that college kids haven't seen and lived enough life to even justify their own opinions. The vast majority of college kids don't know what it's like to fail, to fall, to struggle, to surrender, and to keep moving because there are other people depending on them. Failing a test is no comparison to losing your primary job that pays the mortgage. Failing a class is no comparison to having to cope with the loss of a spouse or child. This is what I mean by stating college kids haven't lived enough life; the consequences and stresses they endure are completely different than those people outside of college. Therefore, to base research on the ideas and beliefs of college kids isn't logical; these kids are living in a bubble of time where they are enjoying the most care-free years of their lives.

In contrast, if this book were to be considered a crude and vulgar form of my own dissertation, know that I formed a lot of my "professional," opinions based upon 15 years' experience as a probation officer. I haven't compiled survey's, calculated statistical relevancies or significances, or even made a cool chart to justify my conclusions. Therefore, the thoughts/ideas/opinions that I offer in this book are considered anecdotal.

However, I have supervised over a thousand killers, rapists, drug dealers, drug addicts, thieves, wife beaters, and gang-members. I have supervised young adults who grew up in gated communities (where a security guard has to literally let you into the neighborhood), and old men living in houses with boards over every window. I've supervised people with a 6th grade education, and people with college degrees and patents to their names. I've supervised people who: had both parents, no parents (raised in foster care), people who were sexually abused, people who proudly prostituted themselves, people who grew up in gangs, people who grew up with addicts, and people who lost custody of their own children. In addition, I've supervised paranoid schizophrenics (one who literally thought that the government implanted a camera into his eye, and that his doctor was part of the conspiracy to spy on him, because the doctor prescribed him lithium, and lithium is what is in batteries, and that the lithium was prescribed only to power the camera in his eye), to entrepreneurs who loved to talk about how they successfully grew their own businesses. Even though this book is 100% anecdotal, I do have a lot of experience, dealing with a really wide variety of people, to base it on.

Please take this as my formal disclaimer: I'm just a regular guy. I am not your doctor, and do **NOT** have a Ph.D. in psychology or social work. I'm not infallible. I wrote this book without consulting, researching, or giving a fuck about the findings of any statistical or evidence-based research available that may confirm or contradict my work. The ideas formulated in this book are simply based on my own experiences and observations of life. I can't guarantee you anything, or advise you to do something- I'm simply sharing ideas with you… If you can't read between the lines, I'm telling you, "Don't get all butt-hurt and try to sue me because the shit didn't work for you."

With that being said; Why write this book? It didn't start out as a book. When I was 21 years old, it started out as a bunch of notes that I jotted down as I tried to figure out how to overcome my thoughts and feelings after my fiancée was tragically killed in a car accident. Then it turned into notes about trying to understand why I was fucked up. Then it evolved into why myself and so many others didn't feel "happy," even when we, by all accounts, should have been happy. Finally, it transitioned into putting all of life's different elements together to formulate a real understanding of what is going on between people and the world around them.

I don't talk about all of the personal shit I endured to learn these things, because this book isn't about "Mark Drake." Instead, it is written **FOR YOU**, by Mark Drake. I want this to be the only book of its kind that you ever need.

I wrote this book in hopes of helping others get through the dark times when they're angry, lost, confused, hurting, or falling apart. I want to make the world a better place. I want people to not only live a better life, but to truly enjoy it. This book is a collection of material that I wish I knew and understood sooner, because my life became much more enjoyable after I was able to learn it, understand it, and practice it. It is my hope that it will have the same impact on your life.

If you're reading this book, know that I understand that you're kind of fucked up, or your life seems like it's kind of fucked up and could be better. I've been there; I get it. Know that I did not write this book to exploit that. Understand that I'm not going to con you with some new spin on the "Positive thinking," bullshit. Instead, this is all of the shit that you already know in your heart and soul, but don't consciously acknowledge. This is the missing information that ties loose ends together, in order for you better understand yourself and others, so you may overcome the burdens that are holding you down.

It is important to understand that life is a journey through the **UNKNOWN**. It's <u>not</u> a trip guided by GPS over paved highways. Everything isn't going to be "Great," "Good," or even "Okay," all of the time. You are going to have times that are chaotic, stressful, hurtful, and fucked up. This doesn't mean you're a failure, or less of a person; it just means you're human and alive! The knowledge in this book isn't going to prevent bad shit from happening- but hopefully, it will assist you to get through it, and to get back on track to a life that is **GREAT.**

Thank you for taking a chance on this book.

- Mark Drake

FORWARD

The "Secrets" that sell millions of books

You've seen these books and programs marketed a million and one times, from Napoleon Hill's "How to Think and Grow Rich," to Rhonda Byrne's "The Secret." They all have some top-secret idea which will bring you health, wealth, and happiness. Ready for the most common secrets, without 250 pages of fluff?

THE 2 <u>MOST</u> <u>COMMON</u> "*SECRETS*":
1) **YOU ARE IN CHARGE OF YOUR OWN DESTINY.**
2) **YOU WILL BECOME/ACHIEVE WHATEVER YOUR EFFORTS ARE <u>MOST</u> FOCUSED ON.**

Part of me just wants to end the book here, put 150 blank pages afterwards, and tell you to write YOUR story. After all, I just saved you a shit-ton of time that would have otherwise been wasted reading hundreds of other books that essentially say the same fucking thing mixed in with the author's own personal experiences. Moreover, from this point on, that's what you really need to think about- **YOUR STORY**.

This book has "Secrets," but the difference is that they are YOUR secrets. In fact, this book is different because it is about **YOUR LIFE**. It's time that you start living it, and make it a life worth writing about. Every chapter is going to have some questions for you to think about, and space to write out answers to. Reading this book may make you "feel good," right now. However, once the dopamine wears off, you'll go back to how you were feeling beforehand. If you want the feeling to last, you actually have to get into the habit of continuously working through shit in life. New feelings are going to happen and stack upon old feelings if they are left unresolved. Stop blaming superficial bullshit (i.e. politics) and start addressing the real shit that has happened, and is currently going on, in your life. Otherwise, you'll be selling yourself short of the life that you are capable of having. Hopefully this book will help you see the bigger picture of life, and act as a guide to help you stay on course to the life you want to live.

"Your future hasn't been written yet."
(Doc Brown ~ Back to the Future III)

CHAPTER 1
LEARNED HOPELESSNESS

Think about a person who is fat and overweight. When you think of someone who is fat and overweight, what's the first thing you attribute to their condition? They don't eat a healthy diet? They don't exercise? Both? The majority of fat and overweight people eat like shit, and are more likely to be found binge watching Netflix on the couch, than they are to be seen drinking water and eating a prepped meal after an intense, sweaty workout at the gym. We all know it- many of us know this from personal experience. This isn't "fat-shaming," this is just being real. **IT'S TIME TO GET REAL AND STOP EXPECTING POSITIVE CHANGE BY AVOIDING THE PROBLEMS.**

The majority of people can accept that people are fat and overweight because they do not put in the consistent effort needed to physically improve themselves. Ironically, however, the same people who can easily accept this ideology about fat people, will balk at the idea that the reason why so many people are unhappy and/or poor is because they, also don't do shit to improve themselves.

Are you pissed off? Not what you wanted to hear? Truth hurts- and lying to yourself about it is only going to prolong all of those shitty feelings that you are trying to overcome by reading a book like this. So- let's stop avoiding the fucking elephant in the room and hit the truth head on!

PEOPLE FAIL TO BECOME THE PERSON THEY WANT TO BE, AND FAIL TO LIVE THE LIFE THEY WANT TO HAVE, BECAUSE THEY HAVE LEARNED TO BE <u>HOPELESS</u> INSTEAD.

Generally, at a young age (between 1-7 years old) people develop an intrinsic belief that someone or something prevents them from becoming what they want to be or achieving what they want to do. Unfortunately, this belief is implanted by someone important: parent (guardian), sibling, friend, or even a teacher at school. Due to the trust and perceived knowledge of the person teaching the idea (intentionally or unintentionally), this belief becomes a core part of who someone grows up to be.

Everyone knows this mentality:
- I grew up poor, so I am destined to stay poor.
- My mother/father was a drug addict, so I naturally became an addict too.
- It's McDonald's fault that I'm fat and overweight
- I will never be able to escape the hood because "The Man," keeps us stuck here.
- People don't understand that I don't want to be depressed, and I wish they would stop telling me ways to get over it.
- I just have bad luck, and I'm destined to fail

This is all <u>LEARNED HOPELESSNESS.</u>

The most difficult part about learned hopelessness is that it doesn't exist in the conscious mind. The conscious mind dreams about what it would be like to roll up to a private club in a Bentley and have the doorman open the rope for you as you skip the long line of people wrapped around the building.

Instead, learned hopelessness exists deep in the subconscious mind. The subconscious mind is continuously running programs in the background of your daily life. It does everything from keeping your heart beating, to driving while you're "zoned out," to reminding you how foolish that dream about a Bentley is, because you're not good enough, and even if you were, "The Man," or some unforeseen event would stop you.

What ends up happening is that the dream about the Bentley becomes a fleeting thought, while the constant reminder of inadequacy and barriers not only remain, they are replayed time, and time again.

People often misunderstand learned hopelessness as being associated to the environment someone grows up in. However, nothing could be further from the truth. Hopelessness is a learned behavior. Your environment will not change that.

If you grow up in a rich upscale neighborhood with a father figure who makes you believe nothing you do is good enough and that you are worthless- then you are destined to fail. This is regularly seen with children of famous/successful people who get into trouble with drugs, alcohol, and the law. Many of them have a mindset that takes every hardship or negative experience as proof of how worthless they are. This creates a feedback loop, that nothing they do will ever work or be good enough. Therefore, they develop a bad case of the fuck-its and try to escape their feelings of inadequacy through reckless behavior.

Oprah Winfrey is one of the most common examples of the contrast. It is widely known that Oprah was born to a poor teenage mother; was raised by her grandmother; survived sexual molestation by family members; and had a child of her own when she was 14 years old (the child died shortly after she gave birth). Oprah had such a traumatic childhood, that no one would ever have expected her to become one of the wealthiest people in the world. Yet, it was her mindset that pushed her to achieve wild success. Oprah used her experiences as a reason to succeed. When she didn't succeed, she kept trying until she did.

Simply consider a middle-class child, who at a young age, is made to feel worthless by his/her parents. Let's magnify this scenario by adding grandparents who tell this child how he/she is fat, lazy, and will never succeed in life. These messages are repeated from the time the child starts talking. What has been programmed into that child's subconscious? **HOPELESSNESS!**

Now when that child fails at something, they are likely to give up faster than other children, because internally, the child's subconscious mind is already playing back a script, "You are worthless and won't succeed." This same child is likely to drop out of school, and never attend college. As an adult, these people typically blame the world for their failure because they feel that the world was stacked against them- even though they faced many of the same decisions and obstacles that other people do. What these people often do not know, is that if they had just pushed a little farther and tried a little harder, they would have found the success they were seeking. Instead, however, they gave up too soon.

Now you completely understand how it works- and you're saying, "Great, but how the fuck do I get over this *LEARNED HOPELESSNESS?!*"

First things first, you have to understand a few other concepts:

1) SUCCESS IS NOT HEREDITARY
Ever hear of Marcus Jordan? What about his brother Jeffrey Jordan? Probably not... But you know their father- Michael Jordan! Neither Marcus of Jeffrey made it to the NBA, even though their Dad owned a

team! They both played college basketball, but neither achieved the success like their Dad. Successful parents don't guarantee shit – just look at Barry Sanders Jr. who didn't go pro, even though he played college ball too. This holds true across the board. Kids might work for their Dad's company, but most don't start their own company that is as successful as Mom's or Dad's. Success is not hereditary, and NEITHER IS FAILURE!

2) LIFE IS NOT FAIR AT THE START- BUT THERE IS NO FINISH LINE

People get completely bent when they compare where they started in life to others… you really need to let that shit go. People feed into their own hopelessness because they have a false perception that life is a race with a "Finish Line." Therefore, if someone gets a better start in life, they're fucked and can't win (because someone else had a head-start). Guess what? There is no universal finish line! You are not competing against the world! Instead, you are competing against yourself. Your learned hopelessness is the biggest barrier to your dream- not where you started. It doesn't matter if you grew up in Beverly Hills, CA, or in Flint, MI, there is no finish line! If you only want to make $50k/year, go get it. If you want to make a $100k/year, go get it. If you want to be a millionaire, great- go get it. You determine the "Finish Line," so the only thing that fucking matters is how hard and long you are willing to try!

3) LIFE IS A TREASURE HUNT, NOT A RACE

Does it really matter if it takes you 37 years to become a millionaire? If you have enough money to wipe your ass on $20 bills, should you be sad and disappointed that you didn't achieve that in your early 20's or at least your early 30's? Fuck no! If you achieve your goals, who gives a flying fuck how old you are when you do it? The amount of time it takes isn't important. You are not racing anyone! Instead, it's about finding YOUR path to success.

4) LIFE IS NOT A GAME OF WINNERS AND LOSERS

Steve Jobs was once asked if it bothered him that he was always number 2 to Microsoft. His response exemplified why he was successful. Steve simply pointed out that both Apple and Microsoft were profitable billion-dollar companies, and asked, "How am I losing?" Today, Apple is more valuable than Microsoft. The reality with life is that it is <u>not</u> a game of football, basketball, baseball, hockey, or soccer-there are no defined "winners," or "losers," just varying levels of success. Somebody doesn't have to fail, in order for you to succeed.

5) YOU ARE THE CAPTAIN OF THIS SHIP

As long as you have the ability to make changes, then you are not hopeless. Don't surrender to being "Hopeless," when, in actual, you're just not motivated. Your life will go in whatever direction YOU choose to take it.

WORK THROUGH YOUR SHIT

Now, in order to get past this internal feeling of HOPELESSNESS, you must build a mantra (motivational saying) for yourself.

It can be cheesy: *I am a wolf. I will weather any storm and hunt success to ensure my family is fed.*

It can be short and poignant: *Failure is no longer an option.*

It can be extravagant: *I am going to make $5 million dollars a year, live in a house on the ocean, lease a Bentley, buy a boat, and send my Mum on the Hawaiian vacation she always dreamed about. I'm going to leave a legacy that makes my great grandkids look at me with admiration.*

It doesn't matter what the fuck your mantra is, as long as it is personal to **YOU** and what **you want out of life**.

My Mantra:

_____
_____
_____
_____
_____
_____
_____

Now, the ultimate key to making this mantra work, is to look at yourself in the mirror, and say it with conviction every damn day! When you wake up, recite this mantra. When you have a shitty day, that's got you down, recite this mantra. When you're driving home from work, recite this mantra. Repeat, repeat, repeat. Repetition is how you learned to walk, talk, and use that shitty computer program at work.

Great- you have a mantra. Now you need some visualizations. The conscious mind uses words, the subconscious mind uses pictures. A $50 printer now has Wi-Fi capability, and will allow you to print pictures directly from your phone or tablet. Find images that represent the life that you want and aspire to have. Print these images out and tape them to the wall that you first see when you get out of bed every day. Some people call this a "Vision Board." Fuck that... This is your **MISSION BOARD**.

What's the difference? Dreamers use a "Vision board," play the lottery, and have an "If I could only win..." attitude. You are different. You're not putting pictures on the wall because you're "Dreaming" about them. Instead, **YOU ARE DESIGNATING THE TARGET THAT YOU ARE AIMING FOR**!

You have a MANTRA that you are going to live your life by, and the things you put up on that MISSION BOARD aren't waiting for you to "Win," anything; they're just waiting for you reach and unlock that achievement. You want to get fit? Find a picture of the body you want, and put it up there. You want a better house? Find a picture of one you want, and put it up there. You want to be the best parent or spouse? Find some pictures of those you love, and put them up there. This is more than a vision- this is your LIFE MISSION. You're not lost- now you have acquired a target to work towards.

Every day- repeat your mantra. Every day- observe, define, and update your Mission Board. Every day- your subconscious mind will slowly begin to change. As days progress into weeks, your subconscious mind will start to erase "Hopelessness," and start to build and record "Strength/power/determination." As the weeks turn to months, and months turn into years, you will find the success you ultimately desire- all while watching others around you continue to piss, bitch, and moan about how shitty their life is. You will understand what it is like to be EMPOWERED, instead of surrendering to hopelessness.

The decision to stop being hopeless is completely up to you. Yes, this seems like "Positive Thinking," bullshit. However, it's not. You're not "Faking it until you make it" either. You are simply deciding on who you want to be, and what you want to achieve, and rewriting all of the hopeless feeling your subconscious mind has been holding onto and using to stop you from reaching higher until this point.

No one is hopeless! It's your decision to keep the hopelessness and use it as a copout, an excuse to fail, or a reason to not even try (or to make a half-assed effort if/when you do try). It is also your decision if you want to take aim, and build a better life.

There is a Latin phrase, *Memento Mori*, meaning "Remember you must die." Build the legacy that you want others to remember! It's your future- it's time that YOU decide on the mindset you want to proceed with. Know that if you keep the one you have, you can't blame anyone anymore- you chose to hold onto it. You ALWAYS have the ability to change it for the better, but that decision is solely up to you.

NOTES

CHAPTER 2
BEHAVIOR

Feelings dictate behavior, and behavior is a reflection of feelings. That's absurdly important to understand, so let's repeat it again: feelings dictate behavior, and behavior is a reflection of feelings. Makes sense, doesn't it? If you are in a shitty mood (angry/frustrated)- you will act shitty towards other people (aggressive/short/snide/insulting). Other people notice your shitty actions, and instantly know that you are in a shitty mood. Feelings dictate behavior, and behavior is a reflection of feelings.

Feelings predicate behavior, but there are other factors that have a significant impact. The first is **OBSERVATION**. The most formative years of life are ages 5-16. During these years, the most fundamental way of learning is through mimicking **OBSERVATIONS**. You've seen this, and probably done this too. At some point, you've probably seen a parent get angry, cross their arms and scuffle away, only for their child to do the EXACT SAME THING when they're pissed! Both the parent and child are FEELING frustrated/angry, and the child mimics what they **OBSERVED** from their parent's behavior. In some households, this is yelling at one another. In others, it's slamming doors. Unfortunately for some, it involves physical violence. Regardless, behaviors become "normalized," as an observed reaction to feelings. The way people behave is built upon the observations of how their parents (guardians), their close friends and family, and the people they spent the most time around, reacted to their feelings. **THIS IS WHY PEOPLE OFTEN BECOME THE PARENT/GUARIDAN THAT THEY HATED AS A CHILD; SUBCONSCIOUSLY, THEIR PARENTS' FEELINGS AND BEHAVIORS WERE "NORMALIZED."**

Think about that shit for a second. Look at how many men grew up without a father figure in their life, only to do the same fucking thing to their own children. Look at how many women grew up watching their mothers endure abusive relationships, only to get involved with guys who are abusive towards them. Look at how many people grew up around alcoholics and addicts, only to grow up to become an alcoholic or addict themselves. WHY? Because the subconscious mind doesn't differentiate "GOOD," or "BAD,"- it just makes observations. Continuously observing the same scenarios makes the shit **NORMAL**.

This brings up the other factor that has a significant impact on feelings and behavior- **REPETITION**. Again, think about it. You're not going to have arms like Schwarzenegger if you do ten reps at the gym. However, if you do TEN-THOUSAND reps, your arms are going to get significantly bigger. The same concept applies to feelings and behavior. Watching a parent react aggressively to their feelings once isn't going to have a big impact. Watching a parent react aggressively 100+ times, is going to normalize the behavior. **Once the behavior becomes "normalized," in the subconscious mind, it becomes a script (like a movie or play) to use when handling feelings from other similar situations.**

Now, let's tie this all together. When someone experiences a specific feeling, they are going to behave how they observed other people behave in similar situations. People do this, because they have repetitively observed that behavior (and/or repeated that behavior themselves) to the point where it has become a normal reaction- as if it were scripted. That's some deep shit… reread this paragraph.

Think about the routines that people go through as kids. They go to school and get picked on and bullied. They go home, and Mom is too exhausted to listen to them talk about their experiences. The weekend comes, and Dad never shows up to take the kids for his weekend. These are the types of experiences that lead to repetitive feelings over a span of YEARS. Then what happens over time? These feelings lead to behaviors that become "scripted," by the subconscious mind. Therefore, when someone grows up and encounters a situation that is close enough to trigger these feelings, the subconscious mind will enact a behavior script which has become associated to these feelings and "Normalized," as a proper response. **THE PROBLEM, IS THAT THE "SCRIPT," THE SUBCONSCIOUS MIND HAS FORMED, WAS OFTEN WRITTEN FOR A CHILD- NOT FOR AN ADULT.**

This is why good counselors will focus so much time and effort on someone's childhood. People will often blame the most recent event in their lives as being the cause (or trigger) of them behaving (or reacting) a certain way. However, there are often deeper issues going on, and the most recent event is not often the actual cause of the problem. Instead, the behavior is provoked by feelings, and the subconscious mind reacts to these feelings through scripts (it made) which were normalized through observation and/or repetition when the person was much younger.

The interesting thing about behavior, is that it can change- for better, or for worse. Why? Because people are creatures of habit. If you change the actions, observations, and repetitions to the feeling, you can change the behavior. Calling bullshit? Consider older people who retire and become bitter.

People are predictable, because they are creatures of habit.

Think about the habits of a retired person. They wake up at approximately the same time every day, and roll out of the same side of the bed. They make their first cup of coffee (and some have that first cigarette), then get dressed putting the exact same leg into their pants first before putting in the second leg. Some grab their newspaper, while others have transitioned to grabbing their cell phone, tablet, or computer and reading the news. They seek out articles that point out how stupid the current political party is, and get irritated, by it. They seek out articles talking about crime in their local area, and get scared by it. Then they check the weather, and just downright get angry about it because it's always too hot, too cold, or fucking raining when the temperature is just right! They make breakfast, and turn on the TV to watch more news which further details how stupid the current political party is, how bad crime is in their area, and how shitty the weather is going to be today. They go out to their doctor's appointments (or meet up for lunch with their friends), and talk to others throughout their day about how stupid the current political party is, how bad crime is in their area, and how shitty the weather is going to be today.

Now, what happens when this routine is carried out for a month, a year, or even a decade? The subconscious mind starts preparing the script for ANGRY and ANXIOUS feelings before it even knows what's in the fucking news!

Many people can easily substitute themselves into this equation like this:
You wake up at approximately the same time every day, and roll out of the same side of the bed. You get dressed putting the exact same leg into your pants first before putting in the second leg. You grab your cell phone and read through social media. You seek out posts that point out how stupid the current political party is, and get

irritated, by it. You seek out posts showing someone who is doing better than you, and get depressed by it. You seek out posts from that man/woman who you have feelings for, and become hurt by it. You get ready and go to school/work, and during breaks you grab your cell phone and read through social media. You seek out posts that point out how stupid the current political party is, and get irritated, by it. You seek out posts showing someone who is doing better than you, and get depressed by it. You seek out posts from that man/woman who you have feelings for, and become hurt by it. You leave work, grab one of the same three menu items from your favorite take-out location on your way home, and eat while reviewing social media on your phone. You seek out posts that point out how stupid the current political party is, and get irritated, by it. You seek out posts showing someone who is doing better than you, and get depressed by it. You seek out posts from that man/woman who you have feelings for, and become hurt by it.

People today wonder why they are so fucking sad, depressed, anxious, and angry. **YET, IS IT REALLY THAT HARD TO FIGURE OUT AND/OR SURPRISING?!** Repetitive observations triggering the same feelings which cause you to react the same way. It becomes a continuous (loop) cycle.

People often think they are "in control," of themselves. They are right, when they are consciously thinking about how to react (like whether or not the situation warrants getting into a physical confrontation).   However, the subconscious mind does have the ability to recite a script on its own. This ability was most likely formed out of a need for survival/self-preservation. If you think back as recently as the days of the wild west (mid 1800's), there were a million ways to fucking die (sickness, infection, predators [humans and wildlife], etc.). The average life expectancy was only 30-45 years for fuck's sake! Therefore, the subconscious mind firing off learned responses to feelings was beneficial to keep alert, aware, and vigilant.

Today, however, we ignorantly live in a life of luxury where even poor people are fat, everyone has access to water, everyone has a cell phone, and anyone can receive urgent life-saving medical care. The average life expectancy today is over 70, and people are now more likely to die of a heart-attack than they are from smallpox or from a grizzly bear attack. The world is drastically different than how it was just 200 years ago. Today, the subconscious mind's ability to use a feeling to trigger a behavioral script (in attempt of survival/self-preservation) has become troublesome- BECAUSE FOR THE FIRST TIME IN OUR HISTORY WE LIVE WHERE CORRELATING LIFE AND DEATH THREATS DO **NOT** EXIST. The vast majority of people are not worried about starving to death or freezing to death. This isn't Europe in the days of the World War 1 or 2, so there is no fear of invading armies or communities being blown up as the result of warfare. We live in the greatest country, in the greatest time, where people's biggest bitch is how a FICTIONAL TV series ended.

Have you ever noticed how fucked up the people around you are? Have you noticed people who have good jobs, and nice homes- but are FUCKING MISERABLE AS PEOPLE? They mope and mourn simply because it's Monday. Have you noticed the people around you who have a real talent or the people who are smart enough to own and run their own business but do nothing other than waste their time pissing, bitching, and moaning about how the whole world is against them? Why are they like this? BECAUSE THEY ARE DISCONNECTED FROM LIFE! This disconnect can be better understood as being in

"Auto-Pilot."

The subconscious mind simply runs "scripted," behavior, thus leaving the conscious mind inactive. If that sounds strange, think about how many times you've actually driven home and then realized that you cannot remember the drive, much less, if you stopped at a red light. Beyond that, think about how you might have had a destination in mind, but thoughtlessly drove towards your work or home. If the subconscious mind can take over a complicated task such as driving, is it really surprising that it can dictate MOST of your day?

Therefore, if you want to change how you feel and behave, you have to change the scripts that are used by your subconscious mind. Some people are now reading this and simply thinking, "What the fuck?" Yet, you've seen this done time and time again, and probably didn't think about what was really going on, or the purpose behind it. Where? Military boot-camp!

Think about the enlisted men and women in the military. They come from different backgrounds (various social classes, cultures, upbringing, races, religions, etc.) and have to come together to form a cohesive unit. The military doesn't simply teach recruits how to fire a gun and then send them out. Instead, it has to take very different "people," and turn them into "soldiers." So, how do they do it? The military reprograms the subconscious minds of recruits through a 10-week endeavor commonly known as "Boot-Camp."

As soon as a recruit arrives at boot-camp, they are stripped of all of their "individuality." Everyone is given a standard haircut (within guidelines), issued a standard uniform, and issued a standard set of bedding. No one is allowed to have wild or crazy hair or to have it dyed an unnatural color (like purple). No one is allowed to alter their uniform or to individualize it. The only thing that makes their uniform unique is the name tag. No one is allowed to have their favorite blanket or mattress pillow top. Everyone is stripped of who they "were," and given a new identity as to who they are- a "soldier."

The next step in boot-camp, is dictating every minute of someone's life. Recruits are told when they will get up, how their bed will be made, what time they will shower and brush their teeth, what time they will eat (much less- what they will eat), what time they will run, march, drill, or train, and what time they will go to sleep. This cycle is repeated every day for 10 weeks.

People ignorantly think those 10 weeks of boot-camp were purely for physical fitness and physical preparation. What most people wildly overlook, is how those 10 weeks of **REPETITION** reprograms the subconscious mind. Most new recruits are more than ready to quit after the first two weeks. However, they are surrounded by other recruits (who dress and look like them) and **OBSERVE** them pushing forward. As the result, most people who are ready to quit, will continue to push forward too. By the time recruits graduate from basic training, they are mentally stronger and tougher than they ever were.

The secret to how Boot-Camp mentally turns different "Individuals" into unified "Soldiers," is behavior modeling through **OBSERVATION and REPETITION**. The individuals look like soldiers (haircuts, grooming standards). They dress like soldiers (specific uniforms). Over 10 weeks, their subconscious minds learn new scripts to react like soldiers (executing commands under high stress environments).

Think this is all just bullshit? Then consider how gangs

work. People are wooed in by the idea of being something bigger (stronger/tougher/etc.) than what they currently are. They are generally beat down (physically by other members), and then allowed to be part of the gang. Once they are a member, they get tattoos and conform to similar patterns of clothing. Gangs use "groupthink," in which irrational (often criminal) behavior is normalized because other members do it and new recruits are pushed to view the behavior as "normal," or "prideful." Think about that; because of behavior modeling through **OBSERVATION and REPETITION**, gangs are able to turn lost kids into hardened criminals by reprogramming the scripts of the subconscious mind, just like the fucking military.

If you want to change how you act and feel on a day-to-day basis, you must first be honest with yourself. It is way easier to bitch about how you feel, than it is to put forth the effort to change. **THIS IS WHY MOST PEOPLE DO NOT CHANGE.** People act like bitching is "Making effort," or "Doing something." Bitching is nothing more than a pity-party. To make matters worse- way too many "Nice," people have endorsed the bullshit: "You poor thing," "You've had it rough," "It's not your fault." **FUCK THAT.** If you don't like how your life is going, then **IT IS YOUR FAULT** if you don't make effort to change it.

The harsh reality is that until you want it bad enough, you will not put forth the amount of effort needed to make that change. Take a moment and think about standing next to a fire. If the heat from a fire is too hot, you will move away from it. You will change where you are per-se. The same thing happens with feelings, and behaviors. Most people will not change until the discomfort (the heat) becomes too much. That discomfort comes both intrinsically (from within yourself) as you do not like who you are or where you are at, and externally (people and the environment you are around).

If you want to make the change bad enough, you will change. However, no one can give you the "Will," to make the change. It sucks to go to the gym in the morning instead of sleeping in. No one can make it suck any less for you. It sucks to save money for your future when your friends are buying dumb shit and partying with their money. No one can make it suck less for you. It sucks to look in the mirror and realize the person looking back at you isn't who you wanted to be. No one can make it suck less for you. **YOU MUST HAVE THE "WILL" TO CHANGE- BECAUSE NO ONE CAN GIVE IT TO YOU.**

One of the worst habits we learn in life, is to lie to ourselves. Lying to other people is bad enough, but lying to ourselves is worse. We often do this in the form of excuses: "I don't have the time," "I'm too tired," or "I'm not capable." Everyone can make excuses to quit. Life is filled with tragedy, hardships, and both physical and emotional pain. Yet, if you would look at what makes some people "Great," it is their ability to overcome adversity to become successful.

People often want to change, but are too fixated on their past (who they *were*). If you are totally focused on the past, nothing is going to change. **IF YOU WANT TO CHANGE, YOU NEED TO BE OBSESSED WITH THE FUTURE YOU WANT TO HAVE. Here are some simple truths:**
1. People fuck up our lives- that's a fact of life. They hurt us, disappoint us, and tear us down. If you FIXATE ON THE PAIN caused by other people, you are likely to continue the cycle and become that very same way towards other people. The subconscious mind doesn't decipher good or bad. Instead, it simply runs like a director passing out scripts. Therefore, the more you fixate on the bad

things, the more your subconscious mind "normalizes," the behavior. The more "normal," the behavior is, the more likely you are to repeat it- even though **YOU** didn't like being treated that way by someone else. Your conscious mind has the ability to override this, but it takes continuous conscientious effort.
2. You can easily give people credit for all of the bad shit they put you through and caused you. However, you must be able to learn from it, control it, and be able to flip it around so you may utilize it, rather than suffer from it. Change your focus from WHAT bad shit happened to you, to HOW the bad shit made you into a stronger and better person.
3. Life fucking hurts. It's going to give you some straight-up haymakers that are going to knock you down. You may lose your job, you may lose your house, you may get divorced, or you may lose a close friend or family member. You have the ability to decide whether the pains caused by these events are going to be the reason why you quit and grow resentful, or the reason why you are so fucking strong and brave that nothing will stop you.
4. You are crafting your own legacy. You can be a motherfucker like your Dad, a miserable bitch like your Mom, or backstabbing prick like your older brother. However, you can **CHOOSE** to be someone completely different than any of them, and leave behind a completely different legacy for your children to follow. That decision is yours, and yours alone.

WORK THROUGH YOUR SHIT

It's never too late to reinvent yourself. In fact, if you don't like who you are, then it's stupid not to. It's time to stop reacting to the life that you have, and start preparing for the life that you want. You thoroughly know and understand that the subconscious mind simply runs scripts that have been written through **OBSERVATION and REPETITION**. Therefore, you have the ability to change if you rewrite better scripts and repeat them as much as possible. However, it takes work- just like a fucking boot-camp. Develop the life that you want. Work on letting go of who you were, and become obsessed with the person you want to be:

Describe the future you truly want:

_____
_____
_____
_____
_____
_____
_____
_____
_____
_____
_____
_____
_____
_____

How do you look in the future you want (weight, fitness, haircut/style/color, etc.)?

___

How do you dress in the future you want?

___

How do you act in the future you want?

___

In the future, how will you overcome failure?

___

You know that OBSERVATION and REPETITION affect behavior. Therefore, in order to achieve the future you want, you must cut these people out of your life because they do not act the way you want to act, they do not feel the way you want to feel, and they do not live the life you want to live (list their names):

_____
_____
_____
_____
_____
_____

What scares you about making the change?

_____
_____
_____
_____
_____
_____

This is why the change is going to be worth it:

_____
_____
_____
_____
_____
_____

This is how you will **CHOOSE** to feel every day, even when the old way is easier:

_____
_____
_____
_____
_____
_____

This is what you will do EVERY SINGLE DAY in order to remind yourself and ensure you are focused on the new you:

_____
_____
_____
_____
_____
_____

NOTES

CHAPTER 3
Happiness

Most people go through their entire lives seeking happiness and never truly find it… until it's almost too late to be relevant. It's not their fault. Most people don't understand what happiness is, and as the result, spend the majority of their lives looking for it in all the wrong places. You probably don't know what happiness is and have been making the very same mistakes.

Presumptuous? Maybe a little- until you realize your understanding of happiness was mistaught, mislead, and intentionally misdirected. It started as an honest mistake, and then was manipulated by a vast array of others.

Shit sounds crazy right? Well, think about how you once believed that a magical fairy came for your baby teeth that were placed under your pillow… What kind of fucked up fairy wants baby teeth? Moreover, why the fuck were you excited and not terrified? Did it ever cross your mind that the little demonic bitch might try to steal the other baby teeth still in your mouth? No. Why? Simple- you were **TAUGHT TO BELIEVE** a specific way. This is why most people don't understand happiness. They were mistaught to believe a specific way.

What is **HAPPINESS**? <u>Happiness is inner peace; a state of mind that is free from suffering and pain caused by</u> **FRUSTRATION, ANGER, DISAPPOINTMENT, AND SADNESS.**

Sounds like some hippy bullshit left over from the 1960's- right? Your mind will reject this insight until you realize that your understanding of happiness is completely wrong.

How did this happen? For most people, it started off as a completely innocent misunderstanding. Think back to the first time you received gifts or presents. Maybe it was Christmas. Maybe it was your birthday. Somewhere in your early childhood (before the age of 5), someone bought you something special, and asked you, "Are you happy?" A young mind doesn't know how to answer that question. A 3-year-old doesn't have an understanding of "happiness,"; so, what are they going to answer? "YES!" It was a gift, a new toy, something special, something that made them **EXCITED**. However, the question posed to them wasn't "Are you excited?" It was, "Are you happy?" What happens is the young mind associates "Happiness," to that new gift, toy, or something special. Through **OBSERVATION** and **REPETITION**, of being asked (and seeing others being asked) "Are you happy?" when they get new things, the idea becomes reinforced; even though it is profoundly incorrect. The kids are **EXCITED** because of the new toys… not **HAPPY** because of them.

However, this hijacked association gets strengthened even more when kids go to the most popular fast-food restaurant where a fucking kids' meal, isn't called a "Kids Meal." Instead, it's called a "Happy Meal." Why is it a "Happy Meal,"? Because there's a fucking toy inside of course! It placates the misconception that "happiness," is the feeling you get with new toys!

As you progress with age, "Toys," transitions into general "Stuff." Think back to middle school and high school. Look at how you thought you would be "**HAPPY**," if you just had the latest basketball shoes, trending clothing style, or other "Stuff," (i.e. smartphone, tablet, watch, headphones, game console, jewelry, etc.). Why did you think that? **MARKETING!**

Just like the fucking "Happy Meal," other companies willingly and knowingly exploit people's misconception of happiness. Why? Because it works... time... and time again. Any product can be a goose that shits golden eggs- as long as it (consciously or subconsciously) convinces ignorant people that it will make them "**HAPPY**."

It only gets worse with age, because the "Stuff," becomes more and more expensive! First, it's generally a car. People don't want a Toyota Prius- because they "KNOW," a Tesla Model X is what would really make them "HAPPY." People don't want to live in an apartment- because they "KNOW," they would be "HAPPY," if they just had that 5,000+$^{sq/ft}$ mansion on the beach. People don't want to be average- because they "KNOW," that having the lifestyles of the rich (who have maids, cooks, groundskeepers, fancy dinners, elaborate vacations, etc.) would truly make them "HAPPY."

Oh... you can't afford the car, the house, or the lifestyle? Then society will try to train you that the reason you are not "HAPPY," is because you need to get a better career!! "Get off your ass and work 18 hours a day!" That way you can spend ALL of your time, trying to make money, to buy STUFF... that will never make you fucking **"HAPPY,"** anyway.

The belief that you would be "Happy," if you just had the right "Stuff," is so prominent in your mind that reading this segment makes you want to instantly reject and dismiss it as being untrue; but think about it. If having all the "Stuff," makes people "Happy," why are so many wealthy musicians addicted to drugs and alcohol? If having all the "Stuff," makes people "Happy," why are professional athletes in the news for assault and domestic violence? If having all the "Stuff," makes people "Happy," why are so many famous actors and actresses known to be complete and utter assholes in real life? Aren't these people supposed to be the "**HAPPIEST**," people on the planet? They sure as hell don't look like it... and they have multiple super-cars, several multi-million-dollar mansions, and triplicates of all the other "Stuff," that was supposed to make them happy.

Look around you for a moment. People today have more now than they ever have (cell phones, internet, refrigerators, cars, air conditioning, indoor plumbing, and conveniences like Amazon, 24-hour grocery stores, and hospitals). Yet, they are more miserable now, than they have ever been. Why? **Because "STUFF," doesn't make you "HAPPY,"!!**

Why does new "Stuff," feel like it makes you "Happy,"? Because it is an **Illusion**! Most card-tricks work by sleight-of-hand, and what you think you see or experience, is not what actually happened. The same concept applies between "Stuff," and "Happiness."

For example, let's say that you had a deadbeat Dad (who you only met once), a Mom who was more vested in finding the next Mr. Right (rather than her own children), and an older brother who bullied the shit out of you (at every inopportune moment). This leaves you feeling sad that your Dad didn't love you enough to be a part of your life, angry that Mom cared more about other people than her own children, and frustrated that your brother, who to this day, won't leave you the fuck alone when you're around other people. All of these feelings are buried in your subconscious mind, and intermittently bubble to the surface of your conscious mind. What happens though, when you're looking to buy something new? You become fixated on it, and all of the sadness, anger, and frustration dissipate into the background. You become **EXCITED**, and you have been trained through **OBSERVATION AND REPETITION** to think of this "**Excitement**," as "**Happiness**." Your brain is distracted from the pain and suffering that it has been feeling, so it accepts this conclusion- "**YES! THIS WILL MAKE ME HAPPY!**" Then what happens? The shit gets old. The mortgage payment on the new house is due. The car has a few thousand miles on it. The new shirt has a stain on it. The mind is no longer fixated on the distraction. The illusion is over, and all of the old feelings of sadness, anger, and frustration return. The "Stuff," didn't make you "Happy,"- it just gave you an illusion of happiness.

Need more convincing? Think about people who go to the doctor when they have depression and seek out "Happy," pills. Does Viibryd, Celexa, Zoloft, Prozac, or Lexapro really make anyone feel "Happy,"? Fuck no. It makes them feel "Numb." Numb to what? **Frustration, Anger, Disappointment, and Sadness**. If you ask alcoholics and addicts why they use, they will often tell you how they want to be numb to the pain. What pain? Not physical pain- but rather the pain caused by **Frustration, Anger, Disappointment, and Sadness**.

By now you understand it. Again, look around you. Notice how people have far more than they ever had, but are far less "Happy," than any other time before. What happened? They stopped working through their shit! Unfortunately, as our world became ever more convenient, so did the ability to distract yourself from **Frustration, Anger, Disappointment, and Sadness**. What do people do when they are feeling **Frustrated**? Scroll through Facebook for hours… as if that is going to resolve it. What do people do when they are feeling **Angry**? They go to the gym, or play video games… as if that is going to change it. What do people do when they are feeling **Disappointed**? They binge watch a series on Netflix... as if that's is going to make a difference. What do people do when they are feeling **Sad**? They buy dumb shit on Amazon and eBay as if that's going to make them fucking **HAPPY**!

The biggest problem is that people distract themselves from the **Frustration, Anger, Disappointment, and Sadness**, rather than work through it. Think about the 1980's. People didn't have the internet. People didn't have cell phones. Cable TV was only 36 Channels, and some of those were still shopping channels like QVC, and government channels like C-SPAN. VCR's and home-movies were brand new and ungodly expensive. So, what did people do? They were left with the option to be fucking bored, **Frustrated, Angry, Disappointed, and Sad**, or to work through their shit and find some resolve so they could sleep easier that night.

The "Secret" to happiness is that it is a CHOICE! Beyond that, happiness is a choice that you must make both consciously and subconsciously. People cry, bitch, piss, and moan about how unhappy they are- but they don't make the conscious efforts needed to achieve **INNER PEACE**, and therefore, to be happy.

You must decide to be happy. There are people dying of cancer who laugh more than people going to work. Why? Because the people going to work get all distraught about the little shit and let it ruin their day, week, month, and year, while the person dying knows that every day is a gift. There are Special Olympians playing their hearts out, while professional athletes (making millions of dollars) half-ass try and then hate on the fans. Why? Because many pros thought that simply making it to the major leagues would make them feel happy and fulfilled (and

are sorely disappointed when it doesn't), while the Special Olympians don't stress about what level or stage they are performing at. There are people who live in small shitty apartments who live fuller and happier lives than people who live in mansions in prestigious cities. Why?
BECAUSE HAPPINESS COMES FROM WITHIN!

WORK THROUGH YOUR SHIT

ARE YOU READY TO FIND HAPPINESS?? You have to be dead honest with yourself and understand that going through this work isn't just a one-time deal that's going to make you feel "Happy," for the rest of your life. If you want to be happy for the rest of your life, you will have to address the **Frustration, Anger, Disappointment, and Sadness, THAT IS CURRENTLY IN IT.** Life is filled with good shit, bad shit, and mediocre shit. Things are going to happen and will push you off your square next year, 5 years from now, and 10 years from now. However, the only way to maintain happiness is to continuously address the **Frustration, Anger, Disappointment, and Sadness, THAT IS CURRENTLY IN IT.** The more adept you are at addressing it, the easier it will become to resolve it, and the faster you will go back to feeling **HAPPY!**

Let's get to it.

List off 5 things you are frustrated about. Don't waste your time writing bullshit responses like 'Politics,' 'Work,' or 'Life.' This is a book- you're wasting your own fucking time by being generic, vague, and dishonest. If you're frustrated because you're not where you want to be in life, fucking own it!!

'I wanted to own my own house by now,' or 'I wanted to have a family by now,' or whatever the fuck it may be! Own it:
1) _____
2) _____
3) _____
4) _____
5) _____

Great. Now start working out some steps you can take to resolve your frustrations. For example, if you don't like how you look, it's steps like, 'Cut out sugar,' or 'Sign up for a gym membership.' If you don't have enough money at the end of the week, it could be steps like, 'Cancel streaming subscriptions I don't use enough.' Whatever it is, just start looking at steps you can take to change it. You don't have to fix the world to be "Happy." You have to change the shit in your life that's got you frustrated! List out your steps to change your shit… start with the small beginner steps:
1) _____
2) _____
3) _____
4) _____
5) _____

Anger is a motherfucker… It is so damn hard to hold onto feelings like excitement and joy, and way too easy to hold onto all of that raw fucking **ANGER**.

List the top 5 people you are angry at, hold a grudge against, or who have deeply hurt you. Be honest with yourself- you're wasting your own time by blaming the world (i.e. the president). The people who have hurt you the most are often very close to you (i.e. Mom, Dad, spouse) or at least know your name. List them out:

1) _____
2) _____
3) _____
4) _____
5) _____

Awesome. Now that you have your list of people, go through them, one-by-one, and work towards forgiving each one of them. By no means are you expected to "forget," what they put you through; nor are you being told that you must continue to allow them to hurt you. Quite contrary- you need to stop allowing them to have any power over you.

When you hold onto the anger, pain, hurt, and resentment, you are locking yourself into a specific period of time. For example, let's say that Dad wasn't around when you were a child. This caused a lot of hurt, heartache, and insecurity. Today, as you sit and read this, you know that you're not a child anymore. Subconsciously however, the feelings don't age like your physical body. In your mind, it's still that child who is holding onto these negative feelings. By forgiving people, like Dad, you are taking the power away from the younger variation of you that has been holding onto the negative feelings which bring you down and prevent you from finding happiness (inner-peace). As you work towards forgiveness, this will free your subconscious to feel more and more at peace with the world around you, and thus allow you to begin to feel more "happiness."

People struggle to find forgiveness for other people- it's natural. First, realize that you are forgiving the person, and not their actions. Think back and analyze the situation from that person's point of view (and not just your own). As a child, you may not have understood how stressed and scared your Mom was as single parent. You might not have understood how fucked-up Dad's childhood was, and how he thought the only way he could be a better father than his own, was to simply not be around to fuck-up your childhood. Realize that EVERYONE is fucked up to some degree (some more than others). The people who have hurt you the most, have a story of their own that you have probably ignored or downplayed because of how bad they hurt you or fucked up your life. There are many times where you will experience things that were not your fault- but it is your responsibility to get over it and, more importantly, get beyond it.

The other concept that you have to truly understand is that **FORGIVENESS** and **TRUST** are not the same! They are two totally different constructs. Subconsciously, most people have a direct connection between the two (i.e. If I really forgive you, I must trust you again). This subconscious connection is what makes it so fucking hard for people to forgive others. This connection between "Forgiveness," and "Trust," is **FUCKING WRONG!** Reread this if you have to: **YOU CAN FORGIVE SOMEONE AND NEVER TRUST THEM AGAIN**.

Just because you forgive someone for stealing your last $5.00, doesn't mean you have to trust them with your wallet. Yet, that's what the subconscious mind tries to tell you: Forgiveness = Trust. Therefore, the mind will hold onto the anger and disappointment because if you forgive someone for stealing that $5.00, that means that you MUST trust them with your wallet. That's not the case. Instead, you can forgive someone for stealing your last $5.00, and never trust them with another dollar. Similarly, you can forgive someone for hurting you, and never trust them to be that close to you again.

Break the connection between Forgiveness and Trust. Anger acts like an anchor holding you in place. Forgiveness, is the way to cut loose from the anchor and move forward.

Truthfully, forgiveness is probably one of the hardest fucking things to do, and some people reading this are probably pissed off thinking, "Easy for you to say- someone never did "X," "Y," and "Z" to you… how are you supposed to forgive that?!" Yes, some people have lived through some traumatic fucked-up situations that they didn't deserve- and frankly, no one ever deserves. Recognize that if this applies to you, the fact that you're still here, and in the fight, is a testament to how fucking strong and powerful you really are.

Beyond that, the fact that you're strong enough to be here, also means you are strong enough to forgive the sadistic mother-fucker, because you're not going to give them the ability to hurt you, and hold that power over you, for the rest of your life. You're not forgiving the action/behavior. You're not justifying what they did, nor are you saying that it was okay for them to do what they did to you. You're also not saying it's okay for them to hurt anyone else. You are simply forgiving them as a person, and in doing so, you are taking the power back that they stole from you. You are not fucking hopeless anymore.

Take back the power. The last step of getting over the anger is finding achievement that resulted from the pain. Maybe being bullied by your brother better prepared you for dealing with assholes at work. Maybe having a deadbeat Dad made you value your relationship with your kids more. Identify good things that happened as a result of the pain which you endured:

1) _____
2) _____
3) _____
4) _____
5) _____

Once you have started thinking about forgiving others and working towards it, then it is time to forgive yourself for all of the dumb shit that you did (or did not do) that you have been holding onto in the form of **DISSAPOINTMENT (a.k.a. REGRETS)**. Maybe you said a lot of hurtful shit to your Mom when you were a teenager. Maybe you passed up college or a specific job/promotion that would have led your life in a different direction. Maybe you stayed in a bad relationship too long or waited too long to try a relationship with someone you loved. Once again, be real with yourself and don't waste your time deflecting this on the world (i.e. I'm disappointed with the idiots around me). Whatever DISSAPOINTMENT or REGRETS that **YOU** are holding onto, list them out:

1) _____
2) _____
3) _____
4) _____
5) _____

Now, one-by-one, work towards forgiving yourself. Look at the situations from a fresh perspective: What was going on at the time? Did you know bad shit was going to happen? Moreover, did you know bad shit was going to happen as the result of your decisions or actions when you made them? Were you in a hyper-emotional state at the time (i.e. in a place of extreme hurt, pain, loneliness, etc.)?

Really examine them for what they were. Write out how they affected where you are now (i.e. 'I'm single,' or 'I make less money.'):

1) _____
2) _____
3) _____
4) _____
5) _____

It is incredibly hard to accept that you cannot change the past- but you're getting there. People hold onto their disappointments and regrets as if they are waiting for their turn in a "time-machine," so they can go back and change them. The problem is that there is no time-machine. The past is set in stone and carrying those regrets will only weigh you down as you try to move forward toward a better future. It is time to forgive yourself, so that you may grow and build a better life. If you don't love who you are, then it's time to make yourself into someone you love. What did you learn from these disappointments or regrets that will make you a better person? Write it out (i.e. 'Don't let your last words be mean,' 'Don't waste time,' and etc.):

_____
_____
_____
_____
_____
_____

The last major hurdle in your journey to **HAPPINESS**, is dealing with all of the shit, that you keep balled up inside, that makes your eyes fucking well up (cry) thinking about. Maybe your Mom or someone really close to you died. Maybe your ex-girlfriend/boyfriend really fucking hurt you when they broke off the relationship. Maybe you just feel "out of place," and deeply alone.

Identify 5 things that really make you feel sad. For the last time, please don't deflect with bullshit answers like, "Puppies at the animal shelter." If you want to find happiness, be legit with yourself. Whatever it may really be, list out the things which have left you feeling sad right now:

1) _____
2) _____
3) _____
4) _____
5) _____

Unfortunately, sadness is a deep-rooted problem and difficult for most people to resolve. The reason why it is so fucking difficult is because there is only one real solution- **ACCEPTANCE**. This is not the answer you want; hell, it's not the answer anyone wants. However, if you analyze it, that's how you know it's true.

We can't bring people back from the dead. We can't go back in time and change what has been done. We can't make people love us. The subconscious mind gets stuck in a fucking loop playing a sick game of "What-IF?" You might be familiar with it- the game goes like this: "What if I said (this differently)?" "What if I did (this differently)?" "What if I was there/not there?" The other game the subconscious mind likes to play is, "Why?" You might know this one too: "Why me?" "Why him/her?" "Why did it have to be this way?" "Why now?" "Why not someone else?" Both games fucking suck because some answers are there, many are not, and regardless of the answers **NOTHING FUCKING CHANGES THE RESULT.**

People will bullshit themselves, "I've accepted what's happened, so why does it still make me so fucking sad?!"

The answer is a miscommunication between your eyes, your mind, and your heart (soul). You don't see someone- your eyes accept that they are gone. You don't feel someone- your mind accepts that they are not there. You deeply miss someone- your heart wants them to return! There is a difference between accepting someone is gone, and accepting that someone is NOT GOING TO RETURN. Think about this: you're gone every day. It's really fucking easy to accept that someone is gone to: their work, the store, the gym, or a restaurant- because you know you will see them soon! Accepting that someone is **NEVER GOING TO RETURN** is much deeper. That's the level of acceptance people struggle to achieve.

How will you know that you've truly found acceptance? You will know, when you are able to use yesterday's tears as the reason why you're going to become a better person, rather than using them as a reason to fail, give up, or lash out. List 5 things you are going to do better BECAUSE of the sadness you have endured:
1) _____
2) _____
3) _____
4) _____
5) _____

As you work through your **FRUSTRATION, ANGER, DISAPPOINTMENT, AND SADNESS**, you will slowly start to feel the weight on your chest dissipate. Life will slowly become easier and more enjoyable. You will **FEEL MORE HAPPY**. Truthfully, this is not an "One and done," exercise. Instead, it's a process that you will have to continue throughout your life if you wish to sustain happiness. New Frustrations are going to happen; address them. Deeper issues are going to make you angry; work through them. People and events are going to disappoint you and leave you with regrets; learn from them. You are going to lose people; accept it and use it to make yourself stronger and better.

The more you go through this, you will lose any doubts about happiness being inner-peace, and inner-peace being happiness. You will see others who used to be like you. You will see people who try to buy happiness with stuff. You will see people who go to the ends of the Earth to distract themselves from the hurt and pain that they hold onto which keeps them from feeling happy. The advantage of knowing what you know now? You will be able to help them when they are ready to find the happiness that you have discovered.

NOTES

CHAPTER 4
Fear

Fear is the ultimate tranquilizer. Regardless of how shitty someone's situation is, or how good their life could be, fear will stop them dead in their tracks. Have you ever seen a deer in headlights? What does it do out of fear? **FREEZE**. Ironically, humans have the ability to think and rationalize, while a deer only acts out of instinct, but both of them do the same damn thing. Why? Because both subconsciously think that the safest thing to do is NOTHING.

Unfortunately, doing nothing guarantees one thing- **YOUR GOING TO GET FUCKING RUN OVER!** How shitty is that? Yet, if you think back through your life, you'll know that it's true. Remember that person you were too afraid to ask out? Where are they now? Not with you. Remember that job or promotion that you knew you should have applied for but didn't? Who's doing that job now? Not you. Remember that great idea that you had and did nothing with? Who's living a better life because of it? Not you.

Fear is natural. It's supposed to keep you from doing dumb shit like falling off a cliff while taking an extreme selfie picture on the ledge of the Grand Canyon, or pushing out a fart while wearing white pants and knowing that you ate Taco Bell for lunch. That's rational fear.

However, most people have irrational fears. The most common irrational fear people have is the fear of judgement from other people. In particularly, what other people will think of them. This is why public speaking is difficult for people; they don't want to be viewed as "Stupid," if they say the wrong thing.

Fear carries over into many facets of life, including chasing dreams and passions. People do not fear opening up a restaurant, clothing store, or a marketing firm; they fear what their parents are going to say about their idea. People do not fear becoming a professional athlete, singer, or actor; they fear what their friends are going to say about their dream. People do not fear becoming famous, growing a fortune, or having a legacy; they fear what anonymous shit-heads on the internet are going to say about them.

How fucked up is that? People aren't afraid of the effort needed to make shit happen. They really aren't even afraid of failing. What they are truly afraid of, is what everyone else around them is going to think. "Are they going to approve of my dreams?" "Are they going to make fun of me for trying?" "Are they going to laugh at me if I fail?"

There is no way to get around the judgement of people… except to do NOTHING. So, that's what people do. Fucked up isn't it? People know that they must actually TRY in order to succeed. Yet, people fear judgement so much, that the fear becomes an anchor keeping people from even trying to move forward and reaching their dreams and ambitions. The subconscious mind tries to play it "Safe," by recalling every bad, dumb, or shitty thing it can to justify the conclusion that failure is the most likely outcome. This further cements the conclusion that it's "Good," to do nothing because it's "better," than trying something and failing.

When you really break down what is happening- it's a SCRIPT. People have **OBSERVED** their own parents be unsupportive or demeaning when they talked to them about following their dreams. People have **OBSERVED** others being harassed because they had huge dreams. People have **OBSERVED** others being relentlessly made fun of because they tried and failed. People have **OBSERVED** shit-heads on the internet be cruel as hell to people. Through **REPETITION**, the subconscious mind develops fear of all the judgement, and concludes that it can't, it's not able… it's **HOPELESS.**

The stone-cold reality of this situation is that you need to get to the point where you simply don't give a fuck about what people think. They're going to laugh at you- **SO WHAT?!** They're going make fun of you- **SO WHAT!?** Have you experienced worse things in your life? **YES!** Do you want a better a life? Then GO OUT THERE AND FUCKING GET IT! If people laugh at you for trying, or make fun of you for failing, then you know they don't truly care about you anyways- so fuck'em. Moreover, when you make it to the next level, you know what outstretched hands to ignore.

If you lead with fear, you are going to fail. Too many times people let the fear take over ("What if?" "What if?" "What if?"), and they give up (surrender) before really trying. If you ever want to live a better life, you must realize that you must keep moving forward- even if you are afraid. Take small steps if you have to, but keep fucking moving until you get to the point where you can tell all of the doubters, haters, and jealous people, "Get the fuck out of my way- because you're not going to stop me." Once you get there, and stop surrendering to the fear, your life opens up… The weight on your back is gone, and you will experience what it is like to be truly free.

The best things in life are on the other side of fear. Your destiny is waiting for you to grow. You will never be able to pull the sword from the stone until you build yourself into the person who is worthy. As a baby, you didn't come into this world knowing how to walk. You fell many times- but you kept trying. As a child, you didn't instantly speak. You mumbled and mispronounced a bunch of shit- but you kept trying. Because you kept trying in life, you learned how to read and write, operate a computer, drive a car, and a million other things that you simply weren't born knowing how to do. So, why let fear stop you now? This is your life. You can go down swinging, or you can go down crying about how you were TOO AFRAID TO EVEN TRY.

WORK THROUGH YOUR SHIT

Name 5 people whose opinion of you matters the MOST:
1) _____
2) _____
3) _____
4) _____
5) _____

Are these people you look up to, idolize, or hope to have a family with one day? **Yes/No**

If you fail, what's the worst shit these people are going to say about you?

_____
_____
_____
_____
_____
_____

If you pursue your dreams, and you succeed, what will these people say about you?

_____
_____
_____
_____
_____
_____

Focus on being bolder, rather than less afraid. It's truly difficult to "let go," of fear. Most often, when people focus on trying to get over their fear, they inadvertently (accidentally) intensify it and make it worse. So rather than focusing on the fear, focus your attention and energy on becoming brave. Think about the little things that you have done and build on them- "If I can do that, then I'm strong enough to do this." Name off some difficulties you have already overcome:

_____
_____
_____
_____
_____
_____
_____

Forgetting about what other people may think or say about you, what's the worst outcome that will happen if you fail? Write it out:

_____
_____
_____
_____
_____
_____
_____

You have to train your subconscious mind that even though you are scared, that you can and will succeed. It's the same thing the underdogs do in the locker room before they take the court/field to play the champions. It's the same thing musicians do behind the curtain before taking the stage in front of thousands of people. It's the same thing that successful businesspeople do before holding an important sales conference. They don't train themselves to be hopeless... THEY TRAIN THEMSELVES TO BELIEVE

THEY ARE UNSTOPPABLE.

Rewrite your "Mantra," from Chapter 1:

_____
_____
_____
_____
_____
_____
_____

Through **repetition** and **observation**, you will reprogram your brain to let go of the Hopelessness. Through **repetition** and **observation**, you will reprogram your brain to let go of the **FEAR**. Through repetition and observation, you will reprogram your brain to be better, stronger, and fucking unstoppable!

NOTES

CHAPTER 5
Addiction

There are three typical schools of thought when it comes to ADDICTION:

School #1: It's the Individual
The original school of thought based upon the belief that the problem is the person- in particularly, that he or she is weak, unmotivated, and should just simply stop using drugs.

School #2: It's the Drugs
This school of thought is based upon the belief that the problem is the addictive nature of the substances that are being abused.

School #3: It's a Disease
The "New Age," school of thought based upon the belief that some people have a "disease," which makes them more susceptible to becoming addicted to substances.

Unfortunately, none of these schools of thought are correct. The thought of addiction being due to the "Drug" or because of addiction being a "Disease," (Schools 2 and 3) are currently the most common beliefs. However, both of these theories are so wrong, that drug use and addiction have soared to new heights since these models were adopted- even though more help, treatment, and resources are available now than ever before.

"It's the Drugs," became a prominent belief during the 1980's crack epidemic. The ideology carried momentum as younger generations started abusing prescription narcotics and transitioned into heroin in the mid 1990's and throughout the 2000's. Yet, nobody fucking talks about the "How?" or "Why?"- even from the 1980's.

Truthfully, people are pretty fucking ignorant to the fact that a big cultural shift started to happen in the 1980's: computer-controlled robotics and outsourcing. Towns like Flint, Detroit, Chicago, Indianapolis, Cleveland, Pittsburg, Buffalo, and Baltimore lost thousands of industrial jobs, and the fallout was massive. As technology advanced, less men and women were needed to operate assembly lines; so, production that once required 5,000 people, could then be done with less than 700 people. General Motors, Ford, Chrysler, and many subsidiaries (including subordinate companies like AC/Delco [Delphi]) started closing factories and saving even more money by moving facilities to other countries. The auto manufacturers weren't alone. Electronics companies that once made TV's, Radios, Computers, and various other components followed suit. People also fail to realize how businesses are indirectly related. When the factories closed, people were left unemployed. In turn, those who lost their jobs stopped shopping at malls, stopped eating at restaurants, and stopped buying their "regular," goods and services. Then the domino effect started and quickly gained momentum. The stores and restaurants where the factory workers ate and shopped at couldn't sustain the loss of sales, and they started to close- thus leaving even more people unemployed. Local governments began to struggle because of the loss of income taxes, property taxes, and sales taxes, so they had to consolidate- thus leaving even more people unemployed.

As factories closed in the 1980's, people started to become fucking **hopeless** because they went from earning $16-$30 thousand per year, to working minimum wage jobs paying $7-10 thousand per year. As if that shit wasn't bad enough, mortgage and loan rates were above 10% during the 1980's; so, when people lost their factory job, they lost their house, car, and anything else that was financed. In turn, the pressures caused family and marital issues including divorce. What's the end result? A complete feeling of **hopelessness**.

Now think about cities that have the highest crime rates. What do they all generally have in common? High poverty, high unemployment, and high drug usage. Shocking… Crack-cocaine didn't cause the epidemic. Crack-cocaine is what people turned to (because it was cheaper than powder cocaine), when they became **hopeless** after losing their job and livelihood.

Not convinced? Millions of people have surgery every day and are treated with sedatives and pain-killers; yet, they do NOT become addicts. Millions of people drink multiple drinks on a weekend; yet, they do NOT become alcoholics. So- is the problem the "Drug,"? No. Cocaine and opiates, could both be eliminated and people will switch to methamphetamine and fentanyl. Methamphetamine and fentanyl could be eliminated, and people will switch to Xanax and Trazodone. It's not the "Drug," that is causing the addiction. Otherwise, people wouldn't simply switch from their choice "Drug," to the next available "Drug." Addicts will tell you that the "Drug," itself isn't the "addictive," component- the "HIGH," (feeling of numb to **FRUSTRATION, ANGER, DISAPPOINTMENT, AND SADNESS**) is what is addictive.

The "Disease," theory is even more flawed than the "Drugs," theory. If you took someone with Lupus and placed them on a deserted island, free of any narcotics, they would still suffer from Lupus. Someone with Lupus could be on a deserted island for a day, a week, a month, a year, or a decade, and they would still have Lupus. Lupus is a DISEASE. If you were to put an addict on the same fucking island, they would no longer be an addict as soon as the drugs in their system passed through. The ONLY thing that allows someone to be an "Addict," is the decision to use drugs by putting them into their body. That is NOT A FUCKING DISEASE. A person with Lupus does not inject themselves with the disease and cannot simply "DECIDE," not to have Lupus tomorrow.

Sure- some ignorant, self-indulgent, whiney-ass therapists, counselors, doctors (especially those making money performing grant paid studies), and treatment facilities are losing their shit, and vehemently disagree with this. They will hold firm that addiction is a disease. Yet- they aren't being honest and acknowledging the "How?" and "Why?" addiction became coined a "Disease."

Crack-cocaine was still rampant from the 1980's, and heroin started picking up steam again as the "Grunge," movement spread from Seattle. Blaming the drug, wasn't working, the "War on Drugs," was a failure, "D.A.R.E." didn't make a difference, so it was time to seek medical help. Yet, insurance companies and government funding required reasoning to pay for addiction treatment. Blaming the individual for being weak wouldn't justify funding. Blaming the drugs wouldn't justify funding. So, they started calling "Addiction," a "Disease," and the funding started to roll in.

The unsavory truth is that addiction is a choice (although a bad choice), not a disease. Drug addicts and alcoholics are not alone. They want to be numb to the world so it isn't able to hurt them. Food addicts want to feel whole inside, in a world which makes them feel empty. Social media addicts want to feel relevant in a world where they feel overlooked. It's not fucking rocket-science, but its consistently misunderstood by idiots with lab-coats. Most of the lab-coats are fucked up socially awkward people (who went into psychology to diagnose their own shit) and truly lack the necessary experiences, with a wide variety of people, in the real world to understand what's going on.

Some will say this is just a vain attempt to discredit addiction. It is not. Addiction is very real and very powerful- but it is still nothing more than a scripted behavior that has been validated in the mind through **OBSERVATION and REPETITION**. Look at how many Americans go to McDonald's at least once a week even though they know it's not healthy. Are they aware that color studies show that red and yellow promote eating? No. Are they aware that they were conditioned (scripted) to like McDonald's as a child? No... What?! Think about it; the kid's meal is called a Fucking "HAPPY" meal, so kids subconsciously associate happiness and rewards (i.e. the toy with the Happy Meal) to eating at McDonald's! Through observation and repetition, the subconscious mind accepts the script "McDonald's rewards me with Happiness." Through observation and repetition, the subconscious mind then repeats the script every time someone goes there as an adult. Hard day? "McDonald's rewards me with Happiness." Don't feel like cooking? "McDonald's rewards me with Happiness." Really busy and a little stressed? "McDonald's rewards me with Happiness." This is why it is so damn hard to order a fucking salad instead of a burger and fries... The burger and fries are associated to Happiness. This is how addiction works- it's NOT a disease. Sadly, many people are addicted to behaviors that are bad for them and are simply ignorant to the fact that it could be called an "Addiction."

The fucking IRONY of it all, is that when you tell "regular," people what they do is an addiction, they have a defensive reaction along the lines of, "I don't (eat, drink, or do those things) because I'm ADDICTED- it's because I LIKE them." This is the EXACT SAME fucking logic drug addicts and alcoholics use- they're just more in depth in their response, "I don't drink or use drugs because I'm ADDICTED, it's because I LIKE the way it makes me feel."

Still pissed about addiction not being a disease? Bulimia (condition where people eat and intentionally make themself puke- which many people mistake as "anorexia") is characterized as a "Disorder." Addiction, is just that- a disorder... Drug use is a symptom of what is really going on. Drugs are not the causation, nor is "addiction," an uncurable "disease."

Here is the ENLIGHTENMENT: School 2 (the Drug) and School 3 (the Disease) are WRONG. The original School of thought (the Individual) was closest to being right, but the approach was flawed. So, it is time to formulate a new school of thought.

School #4: It's the Individual's Feelings
This school of thought is based upon the belief that the problem is people uses drugs/alcohol as a way to cope with or to mask feelings which they do not want, or do not know how handle and/or endure. In other words, they use drugs in attempt to feel HAPPY.

Now there's a hell of a concept! If you have been through addiction, or have been around numerous addicts/alcoholics, you know and understand that general consensus is that the people don't "like," the drugs or alcohol. The only thing they actually "like," about the whole deal is the "FEELING," they get from abusing it. Even though drug/alcohol abuse is a "symptom," of their problem, "Addiction," is NOT the disease or underlying cause! Instead, the CAUSE is the fucking feelings inside people that they cannot cope and/or deal with, and the drugs/alcohol are how they are able to avoid those feelings!

THE UNDERLYING FEELINGS

Addicts and alcoholics want to be "numb." Numb to what? **FRUSTRATION, ANGER, DISAPPOINTMENT, AND SADNESS**. Makes sense, right? It should, because if you read the previous chapters you also know that when you don't have anger, frustration, disappointment, and sadness, you have inner peace, which is also known as HAPPINESS! For fucks sake, think about what Prozac, Zoloft, and other antidepressant medications do- they take the edge off of Frustration, Anger, Disappointment, and Sadness, thus giving someone the illusion of being HAPPY because they hurt less… even though they still hurt just as much as they did before, but are just fucking numb to it… which is the same thing addicts are trying to do… which is why so many of them think of it as "SELF-MEDICATING!"

Yet, this doesn't explain why some people turn to drugs and alcohol and so many others don't. There are three common reasons why people fall into the rabbit hole of drug/alcohol addiction:
1) Post-traumatic stress disorder (PTSD)
2) HOPELESSNESS (Frustration + Anger + Disappointment + Sadness… all at the same time)
3) PTSD and HOPELESSNESS

*Side note: Having other mental-health issues such as schizophrenia, depression, anxiety, bipolar disorder, and/or attention-deficit/hyperactivity disorder increases the chances of drugs/alcohol abuse due to these other mental health issues having the ability to amplify negative thoughts and/or feelings.

POST-TRAUMATIC STRESS DISORDER (PTSD)

In the realm of drug and alcohol addiction, PTSD is very common. Most addiction behaviors start between the ages of 16 to 24, and it fairly-common that the underlying trauma(s) were endured sometime during a person's childhood.

Let's break down what happens with an example. Consider a child who is excessively beaten, regularly, by his parents/guardians. If a child is regularly beaten, they will most often develop issues including: fear of confrontation, high anxiety, depression, or lashing out in anger (rage). These are normal responses to the traumatic stress they endured.

However, the traumatic stress of regular beatings also cues the brain to enact the natural FIGHT or FLIGHT instinct. Kids often learn quickly not to fight back since it typically results in a beating that is even more severe. Therefore, the brain in most children often enacts "FLIGHT (RUN AWAY)," and this is seen with kids hiding under the bed in their room, running away from home, and so forth. This natural run/hide (flight) instinct kicks in like an integrated "autopilot" with the simple goal of self-preservation. The typical diagram looks like this:

A peculiar thing happens if this "autopilot" mode is enacted too often; it arrests the mind at that maturity level (at that specific time and age of the child when the trauma was endured), and prevents it from seeking and developing other methods of stress management/resolution. In other words, if a child endures the traumatic stress of regular beatings at the age of 8, that child will most likely grow up to have the coping skills of an 8-12-year-old much later in life.

Due to this mental arrest of emotional maturity, the brain hard-wires a link between the trauma endured and **ANY** emotional feeling that resulted from it, as it were one in the same. Therefore, in our example, depression will trigger the brain to react as it did when the person was beaten as a child. Anxiety will trigger the brain to react as it did when the person was beaten as a child. Over time, **any feeling that resulted from the initial trauma, then becomes directly associated to the trauma itself.** This will make the brain react as if the trauma (being beaten) is happening, even though it's just a feeling (i.e. anxiety, depression, etc.). It's as if they are one in the same event- even though we know the trauma caused the feeling, and not the other way around.

It's pretty fucked up how the brain can do this, but

everyone has experienced it to some degree. For example: You watch a bad ass movie like John Wick and get choked up when the bad guys kill his dog. It's not your dog, and you know that this shit is a movie, and not real. Why in the fuck are you tearing up then? If someone killed your dog during your childhood, the brain can automatically trigger that association of feelings from childhood: dead dog = extreme sadness = tears, as if the trauma just happened to you for real, even though you are only recalling the feeling because it was triggered by an observation you made in a fake movie.

Let's get back to the original example of the child who was regularly beaten. Now think of this child growing up, and today he is 21-years-old. His girlfriend dumps him for another guy, and this triggers sad depressing thoughts (i.e. "Why doesn't she love me?"). Since this 21-year-old has the emotional immaturity of an 8-12-year-old who was regularly beaten, the feeling of depression triggers a reaction in the brain as if he just endured another beating like he used to receive when he was 8 years old (hence POST-traumatic stress).

Autopilot kicks on- the brain reacts as if it's getting beaten, but there's no fight, and no one to physically hide from. However, the brain still furiously triggers "**Run!!!! Hide!!!! Pain!!! Find someplace safe!!!**" So, what does he do? Many will run and hide (self-medicate) in drugs and alcohol. Why? Because the brain is battling itself. It's triggered the autopilot (**RUN/HIDE**), but there is no **REAL PERSON** to run away and hide from (since it's a break-up, and not a fist-fight). His brain has a problem where the MENTAL AWARENESS of a 21-year-old adult is trying to run away from the EMOTIONAL IMMATURITY of an 8-year-old who is locked in his mind.

So, when these children develop into adults, we see this pattern:

The difference between how children and adults deal with emotional pain is that children try to physically run away or hide from what triggered it, while adults have the awareness and understanding that the only way to run and hide from emotional pain is to be numb to it. In other words, adults literally run and hide from emotional pain through drugs and alcohol.

Now, where this turns into ADDICTION, is through **OBSERVATION** and **REPETITION**. Someone who is beaten might have a parent (or older sibling) who is also beaten and observes them trying to hide from the emotional pain through drugs and alcohol. Someone might start hanging out with "friends," who offer them drugs or alcohol so they can "feel better." Regardless, once they use drugs or alcohol, they notice that they feel "numb," which in turn feels like they are hiding from the pain and discomfort. They then **REPEAT** this behavior whenever they start to feel pain and discomfort. Through REPETITION, drug and alcohol use becomes the PRIMARY way they deal with ANY pain and discomfort, and they become ADDICTS.

<u>HOPELESSNESS</u>

Hopelessness is a trend that has been growing probably since the 1950's. What changed? Time. Prior to World War II, there were hardly any women in the workplace. Now, women are just as established in the working world as men are (Doctors, lawyers, judges, executives, laborers, and etc.). In turn, children have less time with parents, and more time at daycare, latchkey, babysitters, and so forth. Is it women's fault? Not at all. Society changed. Houses became more expensive, and people continuously want bigger and better (and that costs more). Cars have become more expensive. Groceries became more expensive. Utilities became more expensive. Clothes became more expensive. For average people, "Comfort," now requires two incomes, instead of one. That's not women's fault.

The other thing that started to happen more often, as women became financially independent, is divorce. Divorce went from being social "taboo," to being part of the social "norm." Again, this is not women's fault; instead, this is just how the times changed.

Parents spending less time with their children, however, does have consequences. The Golden Generation was able to go through World War II, and readapt to home life. The Baby Boomers were able to go Vietnam and readapt to home-life, but not as well as the Golden Generation did. Generation X was considerably more unstable than the Boomers, without a major war. Then the Millennials became the suicide generation before 9/11 even occurred.

What happened? Each progressive generation had less quality time with their parents. This is the time where parents instill morals, values, model behavior, and reaffirm to their children that they are SIGNIFICANT. Why did social media blow up in popularity with the Millennials? Just look through it! Facebook, Instagram, Twitter, Snap-Chat, Tik-Tok, are ALL filled to brim with people SEEKING VALIDATION. "Tell me I'm pretty." "Tell me I'm awesome." "Tell me I'm talented." "PLEASE TELL ME THAT I'M FUCKING SIGNFICANT!!!!!"

When people do not feel significant, they start to become hopeless. Hopelessness is the magnified cumulation of unresolved Frustration, Anger, Sadness, and Disappointment. With kids it may start with a broken home and a single parent who is working a fuck-ton of hours in effort to pay bills. Then add school-age teasing and bullying. Then add teenage heartbreak. Then add the stress of trying to figure out who you are supposed to be, and what you are supposed to do with the rest of your life. Add a parent, mentor, or close friend who shits on your dream and it's pretty easy to find that sense of hopelessness; teenage angst with a "Life sucks," mentality.

From here it's again about observation and repetition. Mom comes home from work and drinks a bottle of wine to handle the stress. Someone's friends smoke weed and they offer a hit on a joint and talk about how it will help make them "feel better." It's about modeled behavior of someone you like/love/admire to get started. Then it's experiencing the ability to be "numb," to that "Hopelessness," because the cumulative feelings of Frustration, Anger, Disappointment, and Sadness are just overwhelming. Through repetition, it becomes habit, and from habit it becomes addiction. All because people don't know how, or just don't want to deal with their issues...

TREATMENTS FAILURE: CREATING NEGATIVE FEEDBACK LOOP

Many of today's treatments are very ineffective. Why don't they work? Because most of them convince these people that they are POWERLESS (HOPELESS), and that they will ALWAYS BE ADDICTS! Nothing like fucking someone over with a dominant reason to fail. This is known as a "Feedback Loop."

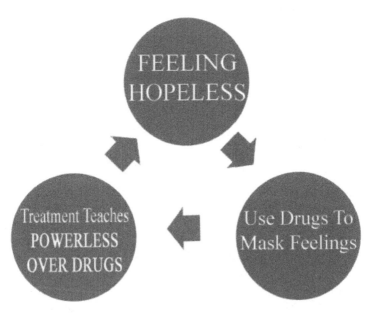

Consider this: Would you tell an 8-year-old child that they

are nothing but a hopeless LOSER? Would you repetitively tell and remind that 8-year-old child that they will ALWAYS BE A HOPELESS LOSER every time they came to you for HELP? Absolutely not! Why? Because if you convince a child that they are a worthless loser, and that nothing they do can or ever will change that, then they are highly likely to become a hopeless loser. Pretty obvious.

Yet, look at how addiction is treated. The first step of Alcoholics/Narcotics Anonymous (AA/NA) reads, "We admitted we were powerless over our addiction and that our lives had become unmanageable." Do you see the FUCKING MISTAKE? **ADMIT YOU ARE POWERLESS!** The very first step of treatment is the equivalent to telling an 8-year-old kid that they are a **HOPELESS LOSER**. It is essentially the same across the entire spectrum of treatment, "You are an addict." "You will always be an addict." "You have a disease." "You will never have power over drugs/alcohol." All of these repeated messages prime the subconscious mind to willfully accept that it is nothing but a **HOPELESS LOSER** regardless of whether someone is 8, or 88 years old.

Again, some people get defensive and want to defer that there's a distinguishable difference between telling an 8 year they're a hopeless loser and telling an adult they will always be an addict. Yet, these people fail to realize how counselors and doctors are perceived to be "Experts," in addiction. Therefore, the subconscious mind gives the opinions of these people more "value," than what someone's own mother, father, brother, sister, spouse, or child could ever say! In other words, an "Expert," telling someone they will always be an addict, holds the same value to the subconscious mind as a mother telling an 8-year-old-child that they will always be a hopeless loser.

The next problem with treatment is substitution therapy. This method is commonly used to treat heroin and opiate addiction by allowing addicts to "dose," using methadone or buprenorphine (Suboxone). The thought is that a medically monitored and "controlled," high is better than an addict using street drugs. Yet, the problem is that morphine and Suboxone do NOTHING to rewrite the behavior script (i.e. bad/unwanted feelings = get high). In fact, the REPETITION (continuous use) and OBSERVATION (methadone/Suboxone makes me feel "Good,") only REINFORCES ADDICTIVE BEHAVIOR. The script is left unchanged: Bad/unwanted feelings = GET HIGH. The methodology is like recommending that an alcoholic just simply switch to wine instead of drinking vodka because wine is more socially acceptable.

THE FIX

People don't change because their Mom, Dad, brother/sister, or children want them to. The **ONLY** way people change is if/when they **WANT** to change. However, it's really fucking hard for someone to **WANT** to change if they think they're hopeless and will always be an addict.

It's time to throw-away the old bullshit (because it's wrong anyway), and give addicts a whole new mantra (sayings or set of rules) that **EMPOWER** them:
1. I want to be happy
2. I make my own decisions
3. Since I make my own decisions, I am in control of my own life
4. Drugs and/or alcohol are no longer an acceptable way to escape how I feel
5. I MUST acknowledge my feelings instead of avoiding them

6. Acknowledging how I feel does not make me weak or less of a person
7. It is okay to feel frustration, anger, disappointment, and sadness
8. I will continue to have unwanted feelings until I address them and work through them
9. Drugs and/or alcohol will delay and compound my pain and will NOT give me the happiness I desire.
10. Just because I was an addict or alcoholic in the past, does not mean that I have to be one today or ever again. I know that NOTHING (including the death of a loved one) is a valid reason to return to that life.

TREATMENTS FAILURE: FIXATING ON "COPING SKILLS"

Yes, coping skills are important and will play heavily into successful recovery. However, there is a reason why simply promoting coping skills doesn't work- **THE REAL FUCKING PROBLEMS STILL EXIST.** Coping skills can be summarized as "targeted distraction." You want to get high? Do something else instead, whether it be something creative, something physical (like going to the gym), or something relaxing (like going to sleep). This approach works because it is slowly rewriting the behavior scripts through observation and repetition (i.e. "I don't have to do drugs, I can do this instead,"). However, it's not assisting someone work through the underlying triggers (ANGER, FRUSTRATION, DISAPPOINTMENT, and SADNESS) which are at the root of it all. Instead, this baggage is just repressed and pushed further down the road. Eventually, these coping skills are not enough, because new sources of Frustration, Anger, Disappointment, and Sadness occur, and are compiled on top of the old sources of Frustration, Anger, Disappointment, and Sadness. This in turn, leads to relapse because the new "Coping skills," are no longer effective.

THE FIX

People have to address their own shit. Regardless of whether it is something petty like getting a toy car instead of a real car on their 16th birthday, or something seriously traumatic like watching one family member kill another family member, the reality is that the internal animosity and unrest will not be resolved by fucking ignoring it through "Coping," mechanisms. Now to be real, there are always going to be good days where people are going to be able to address their feelings and emotions, and bad days where the best thing they can do is to safely distract themselves through coping skills. However, it is ABSOLUTELY essential that any therapy focuses on identifying the deep-rooted ANGER, FRUSTRATION, DISAPPOINTMENT, and SADNESS, and assist the individual in addressing it- and ultimately overcoming it.

In order for treatment to work, it must:
1) Correct feelings of hopelessness by affirming self-control
2) Address high emotional feelings that trigger flight response (ANGER, FRUSTRATION, DISAPPOINTMENT, and SADNESS)
3) Eliminate evasion excuses by resolving them

Recovery is a phase not a permanent way of life. Just ask your local hospital. Men and women came back from Iraq missing limbs, but the hospitals didn't keep them in recovery permanently. Instead, they were told that they have a new way to live their life. They are taught how to adapt to it, and it's on them to make the best of it.

Just because someone WAS an addict, doesn't mean they

will ALWAYS be an addict. The only reason they are an addict, is because of all of the unresolved shit they have bouncing around in their head; they found drugs/alcohol to be the easiest way to run away from it, because it allows them to be "numb," to it. Moreover, because of REPEATED drug use, it becomes someone's "script," to follow any time they feel emotional pain. This is repeated to the point where it became habitual. If you eliminate the "need," by working towards "resolve," in addition to controlling "distractions," addiction can be rewritten with a better behavioral script… or "Cured."

If you are currently an addict, and want to get past addiction, you need to accept that **TODAY YOU HAVE THE OPPORTUNITY TO LIVE A BETTER LIFE.**

WORK THROUGH YOUR SHIT

Describe the future that you want to have:

_____
_____
_____
_____
_____
_____
_____
_____

Describe how you want to look and feel about yourself:

_____
_____
_____
_____
_____
_____
_____
_____

Describe realistic changes you will have to make including associations, friends, family, location, schooling, employment, and so on:

___

Describe the fears that you have in making these changes:

___

Finally, describe how your fears will no longer stop you from achieving the life you want:

___

If you are suffering an addiction, then it's time for change. Don't let drugs become formaldehyde just preserving you in an emptiness where you are hopeless and lost. Don't let social media keep you chained to old friends and old feelings of who you used to be. It's time to let go of the past, deal with the emotions you've been putting off, and develop the future that you desire.

Go through these 5 questions EVERY DAY with yourself. Start teaching your subconscious mind that you are not hopeless anymore because you are on a journey to a creating a better version of yourself. There are going to be struggles. There are going to be feelings that you've been trying to avoid. However, once you get on the other side of those unresolved issues, you will find the inner peace you desire.

NOTES

CHAPTER 6
Depression

This is the point where an editor or publisher is going to make me point out that I (Mark Drake, the author) am not a licensed psychologist or psychiatrist (the title of the book should have made that obvious). If you have depression/issues or just things from the past or present that you know you cannot deal with on your own, set up an appointment with a professional psychologist/psychiatrist immediately. If you find yourself in an even more severe situation, the National Suicide Hotline # is 1-800-273-8255. People are looking forward to helping you 24/7, and I urge you to please call them immediately- even if you're just teasing with the idea. I would rather meet you in person and hear your success story- than read your obituary.

For probably 5-10% of people, depression is a chemical imbalance in the brain that needs to be treated with medications. For the other 90-95% of people with depression, **IT'S YOUR FUCKING BRAIN TELLING YOU THAT YOU NEED TO DEAL WITH YOUR UNRESOLVED SHIT!**

The best way of looking at depression, is like the annoying service engine light in your car- it's your mind telling you that something is wrong! Moreover, just like the engine light, it's telling you that the problem is serious enough that ignoring it is only going to make things worse. However, that's what people often do- ignore it/avoid it and hope that it will just go away… but it won't.

Depression is directly linked to "**HOPELESSNESS**." It's generally a cumulation of Frustration, Anger, Disappointment, and Sadness, compiled over a period of time. This causes an individual to feel completely defeated, and thus produces an overwhelming feeling of

HOPELESSNESS. Makes sense, right? Especially since most people who say they're depressed, describe the feeling as "down," "blue," or "**HOPELESS**,"?

Remember that behavior is based upon **OBSERVATION** and **REPETITION**. When the mind concludes "Hopeless," "Hopeless," "Hopeless," the repetition causes the undesirable effect that is understood to be the condition known as **DEPRESSION.**

In order to conquer Depression, an individual must break the cycle of "Hopeless," repetition. The first step is owning the fact that they are not fucking hopeless! Life is a bitch, and you're going to endure some bad beats, some close defeats, and some hurtful losses. However, just because bad shit happens, doesn't mean that you have to cower in fear because you'll never win. In fact, it's quite the opposite- you need to learn from your mistakes and keep fucking trying.

It's amusing how you can ask someone if they tried their best, they will generally say "Yes." But, if you follow it up by asking them if they could try harder, they will also generally respond "Yes," too! Obviously, if they could try "harder," they didn't give the situation their "Best effort," to begin with.

When depression is ignored, new problems are added to the mix, of what initiated the depression, and make it that much worse. As the depression worsens, a new response typically starts to emerge- **ANXIETY!!** Anxiety is generally the result of the brain panicking due to a lack of "Control." Depression is linked to Anxiety, because people who are depressed often feel that they do not have control (or are losing control), and the brain is reacting in an effort to assist them in trying to resolve the situation.

Your brain wants to be safe and will do whatever it considers necessary in order to protect itself from danger. Because the brain is trying to protect itself from danger, it processes most threats in a "Flight or Fight," manner. Depression is a significant stress on the brain. In turn, the brain reacts to the stress by releasing cortisol (a steroid), in effort to help you fight or run away from the enemy that is causing this stress. This is why people find relief from their anxiety by working out and/or being more physically active!

The problem with depression, however, is that the "threat," isn't figuratively "real." It's a memory, thought, or belief that is being played and replayed in your subconscious mind. Yet, the brain triggers a cortisol release as if it is a real life-threatening person/place/thing/situation that is directly in front of you. If your brain were a souped-up engine, this would be like someone slamming the gas and hitting the fucking NOS (nitrous-oxide) while the car is in park! The engine is doing is damnedest to make as much torque and horsepower as humanly possible, but the wheels aren't even engaged! Similarly, when there is no real physical threat to fight or run away from, your mind is left spinning its gears at an obnoxious rate with no outlet- thus leaving you with anxiety… Ain't that a bitch?

Sadly, it is a bitch, because anxiety with no outlet takes a life of its own and starts to become a self-fueled fire. Anxiety causes more stress; stress causes more cortisol to be released; cortisol causes more anxiety because there is no relief. Once this cycle becomes prolonged, the body itself starts getting really fucked up. The brain is triggering "Fight or Flight Motherfucker!!!" and starts delegating all resources to a fight or an escape that isn't happening: the immune system is being shut down, the digestion system is being slowed down, and growth/repair systems are being idled. Your mind reacts as if you're in the middle of the jungle during the Vietnam War, even though your body might be in the middle of your bedroom in Nebraska- all because your mind doesn't understand the difference between reality and a thought/belief/memory.

This sounds like complete and utter bullshit, right? How can your mind/body not be able to decipher the difference between thought and reality?! When you think about it, it sounds dumb as fuck, until you consider why masturbation works... Think it over- you can touch and play with your bits all day long and nothing will happen. However, if you start thinking about someone while doing it, your body will start to react. If you intensify that thought with visual/audio stimulation like porn- BAM!! Your body reacts as if you're having real sex, even though it's only a thought, and **NOT REAL**!! Unfortunately, many thoughts that people continuously have (or are exposed to) are not pleasurable, and their body reacts in ways that result with depression and anxiety- instead of an orgasm.

One of the conceptual issues with depression and anxiety is that people think that it will simply, "Go away," like a common cold. People are falsely sold the idea that depression and anxiety are (**exclusively**) **CAUSED BY BRAIN CHEMISTRY** and are given the false hope that the depression/anxiety can be "cured" with the wide variety of medications available. However, since most cases of depression and anxiety are caused by thoughts/beliefs/memories, they will never be "cured," with medications.

Family doctors (primary care physicians) should **NEVER** be able (or allowed) to prescribe psychiatric medications. The entire fucking point of these medications wasn't to "cure," people. Instead, they were meant to help people come down from an amped up level (like 9 or 10) to a lower level (like 5 or 6) so they could start to deal with their issues while going through counseling.

Taking the meds, without working on the core thoughts/beliefs/memories that are driving the depression and anxiety, is about as effective as giving blood-sugar medications to a diabetic who goes home and eats an entire gallon of ice cream after dinner… fucking pointless. Without counseling, the only thing the psychiatric meds will do is make your body work harder to maintain a depressed state.

Over time, your body will continue to push the depressed state until the meds quit working. Then people go back to their doctor and get a higher dose or a stronger medication, and the body will start fighting that medication too. This cycle of the body fighting the medications continues; people become frustrated that the meds aren't working, quit taking them, and then are left super-fucked because the body has been working extremely hard trying to push depression and anxiety past the medications. Without the resistance of the medications, people who abruptly quit taking them will suffer crushing lows- and some become suicidal (hence the fucking warnings on all of the meds now about why you shouldn't abruptly stop taking them once you have started taking them).

It is important to remember that in most cases, depression and anxiety are symptoms (warning lights) of a problem, and not the main problem itself (which is typically unresolved thoughts/beliefs/memories).

It's extremely difficult for many people to put in the real work needed to get through depression- mainly because

they have a self-defeating mindset. Instead, of making efforts to get better, people find a million articles on-line (written by other miserable people who have no interest in getting better), and then spread these articles like the gospel. Why?! Three reasons:
1) Justify to themselves that they are hopeless (when somewhere deep-down they know they are not).
2) They are trying to get attention for themselves (**YOU SHOULD FEEL SORRY FOR ME!**).
3) To scorn away anyone who tries to help them to get better (**DON'T RUIN MY PITY-PARTY!**).

Unfortunately, this has created a complete shit-storm. Modern society has effectively killed the old days where Mom, Dad, Grandpa, Grandma, or your best friend would tell you to, "Put your big-girl panties on." Today, most people are scared to say a fucking word because everyone is "Entitled to their feelings." Instead of encouraging people to help one another, a few miserable pricks have made any good person, trying to lift up others around them, feel like an asshole for trying. As the result, many people don't try to help, much less get involved, anymore.

What our modern society does not understand, is that validating people seeking sympathy is like giving treats to your dog for shitting on your carpet. It promotes an endless self-defeating cycle. Sympathy from others becomes justification for the continuation of their bad/poor choices. People's emotional problems (and negativity) are reinforced by anyone who simply says, "Sorry, babe- hang in there," because it causes the brain to fire the response- "YAY!!!! I got attention!!! Yay!!!" Then the brain continues to seek out this attention, even though it's bad attention (pity) and not good attention (praise for trying). The subconscious mind doesn't process the difference between praise and pity, or whether it's good/bad; it's simply running a behavior script which is seeking attention to resolve a problem.

The fucking crazy part is misery does love company. The depressed mind knows it needs help dealing with issues and needs to be called out on some bullshit that it keeps echoing inside. Unfortunately, this simply doesn't happen anymore because social norms have dramatically changed to the point where helping someone is manipulated as "shaming," someone.

The unspoken reality with most cases of depression is that people who look for reasons to justify their negative feelings, emotions, or attitudes, do not want to get better. If you find yourself intentionally seeking sympathy from others, then take it as an obvious sign that your shit is fucked up and it's time to change! Stop making bullshit excuses like, "I don't feel this way by choice," and make a commitment to getting better. The harsh truth sucks: **most people put more effort into microwave popcorn than they do into improving themselves.** Why? Because it is far easier to sit on top of a landfill and bitch about the stench, than it is to climb the smallest of mountains. You have to legitimately want to be better, and then you have to make continuous efforts to move forward until you get better.

WORK THROUGH YOUR SHIT

Make the resolution to yourself that you are done living your life in depression. Every single fucking day, look at yourself in the mirror (or selfie camera) and tell yourself that you are going to be happy. Visualize the future you want to have, and how different you are going to feel. Now write it out:

_____
_____
_____
_____
_____
_____
_____
_____

Stop waiting for the fucking person (or people) who hurt you to come to you and resolve the frustration, anger, disappointment, and sadness they caused you. They aren't coming! Start conditioning yourself to use the hurt as reason to move forward toward a better future, rather than a reason to stay locked into a shitty past. Write it out your reasons to move forward:

_____
_____
_____
_____
_____
_____
_____

Furthermore, stop waiting to be validated by others. It's your life; understand that the only validation you need is your own. Give yourself the validation to live a better life:

_____
_____
_____
_____
_____
_____
_____
_____

Start working on DEALING with your inner thoughts and feelings. Make it a fucking habit to start writing. You don't have to be an author, and this isn't a fucking diary where you drag on about silly kid shit. Instead, think of it as a "Mind Dump," where you're simply clearing out the shit that's bogging you down (like too many apps/photos/junk on your phone). The best part about writing is that you can be REAL. You don't have to worry about your best friend thinking that you're a pussy or drama queen. You don't have to worry about being over-emotional and redundant because the same shit from last week is still bugging you this week. You don't have to worry about being judged because you're so angry that you are crying. You can be yourself. Start working on making yourself a better person. You don't even have to save your writings… Just start working on your feelings that are getting you down and what caused them: who/what/when/where/why/how.

Life is like a bad game of Jenga®; if the foundational blocks at the bottom are out of place and missing, shit's going to collapse when you try to add new blocks on top. With depression and anxiety, it's difficult to add new blocks without the whole thing crashing down. This is why it is important to address the foundation issues. Once you start to address and fix foundational issues, adding new experiences to the top of the stack will no longer affect your stability- or cause you to crash. Write out the EARLIEST event that troubles you:

_____
_____
_____
_____
_____
_____
_____
_____

Don't allow yourself to become fixated on the negative shit caused by people around you. Cut ties with the negative people in your life. If the negative people are related to you, start putting more distance between you and them. MISERY LOVES COMPANY. If you want to get better, and these people don't, then it's time to allow yourself to go your own way. These people need to be cut, or distanced from your life:

_____
_____
_____
_____
_____
_____
_____
_____

Avoid alcohol and marijuana (weed). Alcohol amplifies who you are. So, if you're really bummed the fuck out, it will make you into an embarrassing weepy bitch. If you're really angry inside, it will make you violent. Weed will make you complacent with how shitty you feel and how shitty your life is. Neither avenue is going to bring you the results which you desire. Make a declaration to yourself that you are not going to use drugs/alcohol to escape your feelings:

_____
_____
_____
_____
_____
_____
_____
_____

If you are feeling anxiety, MOVE YOUR ASS. Literally… Start taking regular walks, start doing yoga workouts on YouTube, start going to the gym, it doesn't matter what the fuck you do as long as it is something that requires physical activity. Your body is dumping too much cortisol, which is also triggering adrenaline that is not being used properly (like hitting the gas and NOS button while the car is in park). If you move your ass, you're allowing your body to use up some of the cortisol and adrenaline, which in-turn will reduce your anxiety. Otherwise, these chemicals will build up and the anxiety gets to the point of debilitating extremes. Write out how you plan to be more physically active:

_____
_____
_____
_____
_____
_____
_____
_____

Delete all social media apps (Facebook, Twitter, Instagram, etc.) from your phone. Social media does NOT MAKE PEOPLE HAPPY, so stop bull-shitting yourself otherwise. There are thousands of other keyboard-commandos who will talk shit in your absence- so you won't even be missed. Your absence will only be noticed by your mother, and if she is beneficial to your life, then you should see her in person anyway. Think about all of the negative posts you see daily, write them below, and think about why deleting the apps is a good idea:

___

Stay away from the news. 99% of the shit on the news **DOES NOT DIRRECTLY AFFECT YOUR LIFE**. So why in the fuck are you allowing yourself to stress out about it? Guess what? It's always the same overhyped bullshit! The president (regardless of affiliation) is an idiot; congress is filled with clueless assholes; mosquitoes will kill you; everyone hates you because you are or are not ____ (fill in the blank). When newspapers were the primary source of information, most of today's shit wouldn't be on the front page- and instead would be buried around page 6. Explain to yourself why you need or don't need to watch the news regularly:

Turn off the TV, video games, and internet and get involved with other people. People tune in the TV and tune out the reality of their lives- while they wait for things to change. People often fail to realize, however, that desired change will not happen until they make it happen. Join a softball/basketball/bowling/golf league. Volunteer at your local Church, Synagogue, Mosque, or Temple (or join one). Volunteer at your local soup kitchen or animal shelter. Join an organization like the Elks, Eagles, Moose, Masons, a local car club, or even an improv group. Push yourself to meet new people and avoid being a couch potato. List some social activities you can get involved in right now:

_____
_____
_____
_____
_____
_____
_____

Don't give up. The key to making it through depression is consistent efforts. Understand that the results are going to take time. Arnold Schwarzenegger didn't get jacked overnight; his muscles were the result of consistent effort and training. Likewise, you need to work your brain in a consistent manner to work out the problems instead of trying to ignore them.

Through this process, you're going to have lingering doubts. You're going to have lingering fears. These thoughts are going to try to hold on and continue to trigger depression and anxiety… "You're not good enough. Quit… Give up… Change hurts." This is your mind desperately trying to hold onto a feeling of hopelessness. However, you need to be able to turn this shit around and use it as FUEL FOR CHANGE. "I'm tired of feeling hurt, that's why I'm going to change. I'm sick of not being good enough, that's why I need to do this. I'm fed up with this misery- I WILL NOT LIVE MY FUCKING LIFE THIS WAY ANY LONGER!"

Don't piss, bitch, and moan about how hard something is... it is merely an opportunity for you to grow stronger. Understand that bitching doesn't change your future- it only prolongs the problem. Instead, start to train your mind to see **LIFE AS AN ADVENTURE**. You cannot control people, places, or things, but you can control how you react to them. It's time to live the life you want to have, and that's only going to happen if you change the life that you are living. If you are battling depression, you might have to go through steps 1-10 many times. The important thing is to be honest with yourself- are you trying your hardest? The next question will be, are you making progress? Keep trying- it's your life.

NOTES

CHAPTER 7
Gratitude

You understand what "Happiness," truly is, and hopefully you're working on achieving it for yourself. The next major realization is that the marketing industry has completely fucked up the world by normalizing **ENVY** and **JEALOUSY**.

Think about that for a moment. When you see a douche-bag YouTube star driving around in his new Italian super car, are you thinking to yourself, "Good for him; his career is really taking off," or are you thinking, "Fuck that guy! I bust my ass and can't afford a new mini-van! That's bullshit!" It's pretty easy to understand why the vast majority of people often think the later

How about this though- why do you buy sneakers endorsed by athletes when you can buy a regular pair for less than ⅓ of the cost? Why do you buy golf shirts and gym shorts with the name of some Roman goddess on them when you can buy other brands at ½ the cost? Why do you buy designer bags and purses when you can buy others for ¼ of the cost? The quick retort is "Quality," but do the math jackass! You can buy 3 pairs of regular shoes or 1 pair of "endorsed," shoes. You can buy 1 golf shirt with a giant check-mark on it, or at least 2 shirts without it. You can buy one "designer," purse or 4 knock-offs. Even if the quality was shit in comparison (which it rarely is now that computer-automation does most of the work, and you're able to return almost anything- even if you buy it on-line), the simple fact that you can get multiples negates what little "Quality," difference there may be. This is further exemplified when you simply consider the PURPOSE of the actual item itself. Shoes get walked/ran in. Shorts get sweated in. Purses hold shit… End of story. The REAL reason people blow their money on big name shit isn't "Quality," it's STATUS; the fixation on "What do others think of me?"

Owning a 7-bedroom/8.5-bathroom, 6,000 square/feet house makes sense if you have a fuck-ton of kids, or have multiple generations living under the same roof. Hell, it even makes sense if you're running a bed and breakfast or renting out rooms by the month. However, that's rarely the case. You see people who own these homes, and they're generally a couple with maybe two kids. So, what's the fucking point of having the other 4 bedrooms? STATUS (What do others think of me?).

Why is STATUS so fucking important to people? Because they have all been brainwashed to think that it is important. By giving extreme relevancy to STATUS, not only can companies sell you overpriced handbags and gym gear, then they can sell you $1,000+ suits, $10,000+ watches, $500,000+ sports cars, and $1,000,000+ houses that you have ZERO FUCKING NEED FOR!!

In all reality- does anyone know what brand your $1,000+ suit is if you don't tell them? Fuck no. Does that $10,000 watch do anything special? HELL NO! It keeps time… the same thing that a shitty Dollar-Store watch does. How about a $500,000 sports car? Well, considering that there are speed-limits throughout the country, you'll have to take the car to a race track to really see what it can truly do, and for most people, they're not going to take the chance of wrecking the son-of-a-bitch just to find out. Therefore, again, it's a fucking waste of money. Yet, as dumb as it is when you break it all down, people still want it all, simply because of the STATUS associated to it.

Most people can comprehend that, but it still doesn't

change their mind. The marketing industry has brainwashed people by playacting their subconscious desires of ENVY and JEALOUSY. How? By planting images: Imagine how ENVIOUS your friends will be of you if you own this mansion; Imagine how JEALOUS your friends will be if you owned this car; Imagine how your friends will wish they were you because you wear this watch or this suit. YOU CAN'T AFFORD THIS SHIT? Then you should be ENVIOUS of people who own a mansion like this; You should be JEALOUS that you cannot buy this car; If you want to be important, then you want to be the person who wears this watch or this suit. THIS HAS BECOME THE FUCKING "NORM," OF OUR SOCIETY!

It's easy to get trapped in the mindset that what you have is "NOT GOOD ENOUGH." Moreover, once you get stuck in this mindset, you get trapped in misery. In this state of misery, the mind starts seeking other miserable people, just to justify its own misery, and in-turn, make itself feel better about where it's at; hence, "MISERY LOVES COMPANY." People are easily attracted to the misery and misfortune of others- just like bugs to the light of a fly zapper (just think of the traffic jams that occur over people gawking at a car accident on the other side of the fucking road!). Unfortunately, misery makes people even more susceptible to chase STATUS. This is where people start maxing out credit-cards or shoplifting in hopes of achieving STATUS through desirable things (even though they can't afford them).

Still need more convincing? What is the common term for a post on social media? "STATUS UPDATE" (Mic Drop mother fucker). Think about the most common shit that people post about on social media, "I'm going on vacation here," "I have a wonderful family," "I bought a new house/car/high priced (thing)," "I'm getting married,"

"We're having kids," "I'm getting a promotion." It's all shit that no one honestly gives a fuck about- unless you're that person's parent or best friend. So, why is social media filled with the shit? Fucking STATUS.

Sadly, STATUS is just clever marketing, selling you SHIT THAT YOU DO NOT NEED, to impress people THAT YOU DO NOT EVEN CARE ABOUT! Its time to WAKE THE FUCK UP, and realize: "WHO GIVES A FUCK?" Gina isn't impressed with your 3-bedroom 1,800 $^{sq/ft}$ house; who gives a fuck what Gina thinks?! Is she paying the mortgage? Tommy isn't impressed with your 5-year-old car that is paid off; who gives a fuck what Tommy thinks?! Is Tommy going to buy your next car? Heather isn't impressed with your Timex watch; well Heather should watch herself. James is embarrassed that you're wearing clothes without designer tags. Is your shit clean and tidy? Is it appropriate for the occasion (i.e. suit for wedding/funeral, polo and dress slacks for business casual)? Then James better stop clowning, 'cause it's not like you're dressed to work at the fucking circus.

It is difficult to overcome the subconscious brainwashing that you have endured up until this point which has made people so fixated on STATUS and WHAT OTHER PEOPLE THINK. However, the cure is simple: **GRATITUDE**. When you take a giant step back, and realize what you have, it begins to minimalize the importance of STATUS. Once you are able to become grateful for what you have, it eliminates the jealousy that you have of others and the envy you seek from others.

Starting first thing in the morning, go throughout your day by being conscious of elements in your life which you are grateful for. Be grateful for the bed you're sleeping in, because you're not on the floor. Be grateful for that hot shower, as some people do not have heated water. Be grateful to be able to have such an abundance of water, that you can literally shit in it, and flush it away, as there are people around the world who walk miles just to get drinking water! Be grateful for the ability to work for decent money and afford luxuries like a car or fast food, as there are areas where there are no jobs, much less jobs that would afford you luxuries that you take for granted (i.e. your cell phone with internet). As you build gratitude throughout the day, you will find your mindset changing. Do this for a week, a month, a season, or an entire year, and you will have an entirely different outlook on life.

Why does this work? Because it is reprogramming the subconscious mind to be HUMBLE instead of running on the notion that your life and what you have is "NOT GOOD ENOUGH," based on STATUS. Gratitude pushes the subconscious mind out of the "Misery Loves Company," complex that is looking to tear down the world out of JEALOUSY, and into a realm of stability as it accepts that happiness is not dependent upon your STATUS in comparison to others, or the fortunes or misfortunes they endure. It sounds like typical "Power of Positive Thinking," bullshit. However, **GRATITUDE** alleviates stress and thereby amplifies inner peace- the feeling of happiness.

Now some people are going to get pissy, and state that their life is shit, and they don't have ANYTHING to be grateful for. Truthfully- you do. You're still breathing, and as long as you're breathing, you have the ability to change course, and make a better life, as you proceed in a new direction. "BAD," things are going to happen to you and to those you love and care about- that's life. However difficult those times may be, they add colors to the pallet of life, and will give you a new perspective. The hard times aren't as bad when you focus on the fact that you have lived through worse. You have the ability to treasure the good times and good relationships more, when you've been through bad times and bad relationships.

Positive change doesn't happen by accident. It's something you have to want. It's something you have to seek out and work towards. No one is going to hand it to you, and you will die without achieving your best life if you idly wait and do nothing. Give appreciation and gratitude, as they will help you weather the storms of life, and help you keep balanced and focused on what is truly important.

WORK THROUGH YOUR SHIT

Write out 5 things you have always wanted and considered to be game changers if you actually had them:
1)_____
2)_____
3)_____
4)_____
5)_____

Now, think about what those things will actually change. Will they truly make life easier or better? Do you want them for what they can do, or only for the STATUS of owning them?

_____
_____
_____
_____
_____
_____
_____
_____

Write out 5 things you already own, that someone in a remote third-world country would be jealous of:
1) _____
2) _____
3) _____
4) _____
5) _____

Think about those things. How do they make your life easier or better? Do you want them for what they can do, or for the STATUS of owning them?

_____
_____
_____
_____
_____
_____
_____
_____

Gratitude isn't simply limited to "stuff," that you have. It can also include relationships, experiences, opportunities, and even future plans. Take a minute to write out 5 other things you are grateful for at this moment:

1) _____
2) _____
3) _____
4) _____
5) _____

Think about how these experiences and relationships have made you a better person. Is STATUS really important? Why or why not?

_____
_____
_____
_____
_____
_____
_____
_____

NOTES

CHAPTER 8
Relationships

Buckle-up, there are going to be some bumpy roads in your future, and many of them are (and will be) caused by the relationships in your life. Part of being human, is becoming close to other people. In turn, you will experience some of the greatest moments of being alive, and some of the most emotionally painful experiences of your life as well. This is how life works. There is no way to avoid the negative aspects of it and only have joyful experiences; life doesn't work that way.

The first thing to truly understand about relationships is that they are **NOT** all the same. Some people **SHOULD** be closer to you than others. We'll illustrate this with the following diagram:

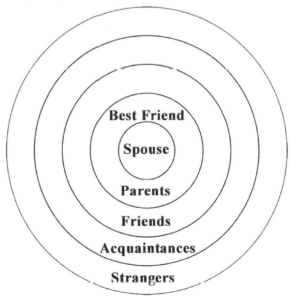

In today's modern age of social media however, boundaries have become dramatically blurred. There are elements of your personal life that shouldn't be open to everyone. However, people get fucked-up because their subconscious mind takes the idea of a "**STATUS UPDATE**," way to literally. Just because you have a shit-ton of friends/followers online, doesn't give you "Status," per se. Furthermore, posting every fucking detail about your life doesn't build your "Status," either. Many people do not think about the consequences when they share way too much personal information with people who truly should not be privileged knowing it- much less, to have access to it.

Aside from the obvious harassment/blackmail, there are other consequences of sharing personal information about your life- you are directly soliciting input from people who do not know you very well, and may not have your best interest/wellbeing in heart. Yet, because they give you input/feedback/"Comments"/likes/hearts, the subconscious mind starts to give these people VALUE, as if they are truly important people in your life. The longer this continues, the more and more value the subconscious mind gives them, and the more it seeks feedback/comments/likes. In turn, people start changing who they are, and what they are willing to do, not based on the opinions of people who truly care, but instead because of people they barely know, if at all.

Now instead of relationships looking like the previous graphic, they look more like the following graphic:

This is easily seen with how much people **VALUE** the thoughts and opinions of people who are not significant and **REALLY DO NOT MATTER!** Look at how easy it is to get butt-hurt because some acquaintance from high school talks shit about you. You might have had classes with the person, but they weren't in your clique back then, and weren't really your "Friend." So, why in the fuck does their opinion matter to you now? It shouldn't. Today, however, social boundaries have eroded so much that they know every fucking thing about you- including how to hurt your feel-bads.

Today this goes well beyond just old high school people. Now you can get shit from some asshole who is simply a "friend," of your "friend," Robert, Jenny, John, or Mary. You don't even have to know these pricks, and some of them will try to cut you deep with their insults. Moreover, they know how to, because you have shared more information through social media, than you would have if you were face-to-face with your best friend.

That is the value of boundaries. Boundaries give you the ability to **SUBCONSCIOUSLY** recognize whose opinion is valuable and valid, and whose opinion is about as worthless as dog shit on a humid summer day. Why "subconsciously," you ask? Because that's the part of the brain that lets stupid shit fester to the point where it brings you down.

For the sake of becoming your best-self, it is really fucking important to identify toxic people in your world and get them OUT of your life. Social media is a great place to start because it is really an impersonal platform. Ideally, the best thing to do would be to unplug from social media altogether (at least take the apps off your phone and only use a secondary device like a tablet or computer at home, so you don't have instant 24-hour access to it). If you cannot unplug from social media altogether, at least start by "unfollowing," "unfriend," or "block," all of the people who do nothing but troll for attention and/or piss people off. Next, do the same thing to the people who do nothing but piss, bitch, and moan- especially the ones that constantly do it about news and politics (even if you agree with them). Now go through your own posts and shit, and delete anything personal or negative (especially if it is something that you wouldn't show to a complete stranger that you just met yesterday). By going through your own shit, you will see what kind of "friend," you are perceived to be (i.e. positive, negative, seeking attention, etc.).

After you get some practice on social media, it's time that you start looking at real relationships that you have with people around you- i.e. significant other, parents, best friend, work/school-friends, acquaintances, and so forth. Understand that it is completely normal to have different levels of trust with these people! There is shit you can talk about with your significant other that doesn't need the approval of your parents (like buying a house/car/having kids). There is shit you can talk about with your parents that your friends don't need to know about (like your insecurities). Different people are going to have different levels of trust. This is unique to every person. Some people might have trust that looks like the graphic below, and there is nothing wrong with that!

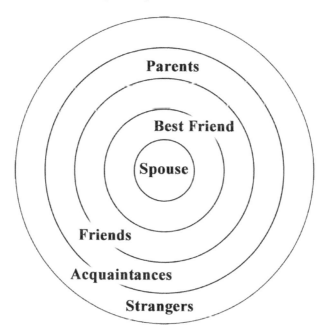

Accept the fact that where family members stand in your life is NOT important. Just because your Mom and Dad got it on in a cheap hotel room, and physically made you, doesn't make them "good," or "dependable," people. In a perfect world, titles like Mom/Dad, brother/sister, aunt/uncle, cousin would dictate how close you are to someone. Guess what? Life's not perfect. If your Mom is less dependable that your best friend, then it's okay to be closer to your best friend than you are to your own mother. If your brother is a back-stabbing little bitch that would steal your last $20, then it's okay to be closer to regular friends than you are to your own flesh-n-blood brother. Blood-relation doesn't entitle anyone to anything. If someone treats you like shit, it's okay to distance yourself from them, regardless of who the fuck they are. This is your fucking life- therefore only you know who truly cares, loves you, and looks-out for you.

Moving forward, you must accept that **PEOPLE WILL NOT CHANGE** because you want them to, asked them to, or even begged them to. **YOU MUST ACCEPT PEOPLE FOR WHO THEY ARE- AND ADJUST YOUR BOUNDARIES ACCORDINGLY**. The pessimistic woman who you called "Mom," isn't going to become some radiantly optimistic person because you want her to be. The unreliable spouse that you married isn't likely to get their shit together because you stayed up for nights on end and begged them to change. The best friend you had since high school who now isn't returning your text messages or phone calls isn't likely to become your best friend again like the old days. **ACCEPT PEOPLE FOR WHO THEY ARE- AND ADJUST YOUR BOUNDARIES ACCORDINGLY...** even if that means moving on without them.

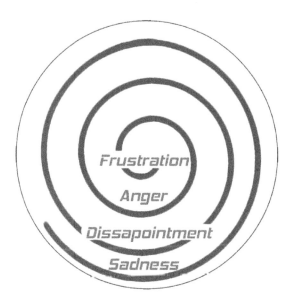

If you really want to be **HAPPY** in your relationships, observe how people make you feel. The more **ANGER, FRUSTSTRATION, DISAPPOINMENT, AND SADNESS** someone brings to your life, the further away you should keep them- like the outward turning spiral in the graphic above. When you pay attention to how people make you feel, they will mostly classify themselves in your life. The hardest part is just being honest with yourself as people become accustomed to making excuses to keep bad people close (i.e. that's my Mom, he/she's always been that way, we've been friends forever, etc.). One of the biggest lessons you will learn in life is **PEOPLE WILL TREAT YOU HOW YOU ALLOW THEM TO TREAT YOU.** In other words, if you allow people to walk on you like a doormat, then they will keep doing it. If you don't like being treated like shit, then push these people towards your outer rings and stop letting them.

Social media has bastardized the idea of "friends." Just because you know who someone is, or you mutually "follow" each other, doesn't make you "friends,"- those are called "Acquaintances." If you have trouble differentiating whether someone is a real "friend," look at their intentions. Your "friends," are the people who encourage you to become your best and help you chase your dreams. They won't simply kiss your ass and agree with dumb ideas like opening up an ice-cream stand in the Arctic Circle. A real friend will encourage you to open an ice-cream stand someplace warmer than 32 degrees 6 months out of the year, or suggest that you sell other deserts so you can financially make it through the winter months. Friends want you to succeed. Acquaintances will talk shit behind your back- like how fucking dumb your ice-cream stand dream is. Misery loves company- but holds no loyalty.

The next big stumbling block people have is seeking affirmations and validations. People today are kind of fucked up because they have been awarded with participation ribbons and trophies since they were kids. People have hundreds (if not thousands) of friends online that senselessly hit a "like," button to anything they post about their personal life. As the result of an abundance of meaningless praise, people have become fucked up with emotionally insecurities. More and more people are struggling to decipher legitimate accolades from meaningless recognition. There are literally people who get down and depressed if their social media posts don't get 50, 100, or 1,000 "likes,"! Think about that shit! Check yourself- **WHO THE FUCK ARE YOU TRYING TO IMPRESS, AND WHY DOES IT REALLY MATTER?**

Now some people have a more "legitimate" gripe in looking for affirmation and validation. It is completely natural to look for recognition and praise from a parent. This is what you were trained to do as a child: "I got an 'A' Mommy!" "You're so smart Johnny!" However, that shit is supposed to stop when you're an adult.

As adults, this issue develops into a two-pronged problem: 1) The parents who never gave affirmation and/or validation, and 2) The parents who don't transition out of their "parental role," per-se. Kids who never received proper affirmation and validation from their parents will often grow up and mindlessly seek it for the rest of their adult life. This continues until they understand, and at some point, willingly accept that they do not need it anymore. Moreover, even if they were to get the affirmation/validation later in life (i.e. in their 20's, 30's, or 40's), it really isn't going to mean shit anyway- because in scale, it will seem and feel like a sparkler when they deserve a 4th of July showcasing of fireworks. It's time to stop looking for affirmation/validation. Even though you may have started life doing things for someone else, **NOW YOU ARE DOING IT FOR YOURSELF**- fuck the rest of them.

The second group of people are adults who were babied/coddled too much, instead of being pushed to be independent. Everyone knows someone like this- they cannot take a shit without calling Mommy to make sure it's ok first, because the bathroom they want to use doesn't have the right brand of toilet-paper. However, if Mommy says it's ok, then they can do anything. This group needs to understand that **LIFE'S LESSONS ARE LEARNED THROUGH MISTAKES.** It is great that they had a parent(s) who loved them so much that they went to extremes to ensure nothing bad happened to them. However, parents failed their duties if their child did not mature into an **INDEPENDENT** adult!

Now that really seems like some asshole shit to say, right? But when you think about it, you will see that it's the fucking truth that no one else will tell you. As an adult, it's ok to ask for advice from a parent. However, if you are seeking their validation/affirmation then you are completely fucking yourself over. This is **YOUR LIFE** to live- and no one else's. You must make decisions based on what you know in your heart and mind is best. You cannot base all of your decisions on what your parents think is best.

Moving along, let's address the most common "problemed," relationships- romantic relationships and marriage. A smart man once said the secret to a long marriage was simple- don't get divorced. After three divorces though, he didn't have any advice to give about how to make a "happy," marriage. Fortunately, you're not talking to him, and you have this book instead. The "secret," to a "happy marriage," is simple- **DON'T EXPECT THE OTHER PERSON TO MAKE YOU HAPPY!** Yes, that sounds fucked up- but the truth often isn't what you want to hear.

Many people get involved in a relationship, and the initial excitement distracts them from the stresses they hold inside (thus giving them the feeling of happiness). Over time however, these stresses bubble to the surface and one person thinks, "I can fix him/her," and the other person thinks, "He/she should make me happy." Both ideas are profoundly ignorant, but people stay in these relationships until they go nuclear, and into meltdown.

Unless you're one hell of a psychologist, you're not going to "fix," the other person. Beyond that, the other person must **WANT** to change first. Unfortunately, the path of least resistance is to deflect change. It's easier for people to blame the person who is trying to change them (regardless of their intent), rather than addressing the issues which prevent them from being happy with themselves.

To expect someone to make you happy, without actively working on the stresses which prevent you from obtaining it on your own, is simply an unrealistic expectation. You are requiring the other person to sacrifice any hope they have of achieving their own happiness to appease you! Think about it- the stress of having to constantly distract someone from all of their internal pain, that they don't want to deal with, will cause the other person to experience anger, frustration, disappointment, and ultimately, sadness.

Romantic relationships are like a layered cake (which kind of gives a wedding cake more symbolism)- you have two layers of cake (symbolic of two people in courtship), merged together as one "cake," with frosting (symbolic of happiness holding the two layers together). Now, imagine that one of the layers is completely perfect, and the other layer is burnt to a fucking crisp. The frosting on the cake will not change the fact that it still tastes like shit as far as cakes are concerned. Relationships are fairly similar. Even if one person is perfect, while the other person is completely fucked up, they are not going to be able to generate enough happiness together to make the relationship work. Happy relationships require two people who are happy, on their own, so the happiness between them compliments the relationship and fills in minor imperfections between them.

If you asked people why they got divorced, the first answer is generally "Money," and the second answer is how they weren't "Happy," anymore. Money is more of a generic "I don't want to tell you personal shit about my life," response. However, there is some truth beneath it. What do unhappy people do? Try to distract themselves. How do they distract themselves? By buying dumb shit even if they can't afford it. "Un-Happiness," is truly the most legitimate reason why people get divorced.

Let's digress for a moment. When people are looking to get into a serious or committed relationship, what are they always told they should look for? **SOMEONE WHO MAKES THEM "HAPPY."** Now, assuming you've read the book up until this point, you understand that "Happiness," isn't something that can be given or supplied to you- it is the feeling you have in the absence of Frustration, Anger, Disappointment, and Sadness. Therefore, telling people they should seek someone who "makes them happy," is fucking terrible advice because it is completely unrealistic and unobtainable. Someone can distract you from your frustration, anger, disappointment, and sadness and give you the illusion of feeling "happy," but even the best magician won't be able to distract you after you've seen the same trick 1,000+ times.

Have you ever considered why people cheat? Infidelity generally happens when one person isn't "happy," in the relationship and becomes involved with someone who they perceive to "make them happy." The problem is that the affair never really "made," the cheater "happy," per-se, but just like buying dumb shit, served as a distraction. That "distraction," gives them the illusion of happiness. The majority of people who cheat don't find sustained happiness with the person they have an affair with. Even if they start a relationship with that person, the relationship quickly dissolves just like their original marriage did. Cheaters bounce from one relationship to the next, always looking at how the grass is greener on the other side, before ultimately realizing that there is no "Greener." They are all just different shades of green. Moreover, the problem isn't with their partner, the problem is within themselves! Yet, until they address their own problems, they will never find sustained "Happiness," with anyone.

Getting back on topic, the secret to a "Happy," marriage is **NOT EXPECTING THE OTHER PERSON TO "MAKE," YOU HAPPY.** You have to want to be happy. As previously discussed, if you want to be happy, you must resolve your Frustration, Anger, Disappointment, and Sadness (the baggage you brought with you into the relationship). Now, the harder part of a successful "Happy," marriage, is to get your partner to take the same approach, and to truly work through their own shit, rather than expecting you to distract them. Many relationships don't work out because the individuals, by themselves, are not happy on their own. Each and every relationship is subjective, and breaking points will vary for everyone.

The true irony of relationships is the advice that people give others who are rebounding from a fresh breakup: "Take some time and work on yourself." "You need to cope and work through your pain before jumping into your next relationship." "**You have to be happy with yourself, before you look for someone else**." Where the fuck was this advice when you first started dating?! Notice how the advice after the breakup is so **MUCH BETTER** than the advice you first received (i.e. "Find someone who will make you happy.")? Life is cruel sometimes…

WORK THROUGH YOUR SHIT

Start thinking about the people who are close to you. Figure out where they belong in the graphic below. Keep in mind that people who prevent you from being happy (because they bring Frustration, Anger, Disappointment, and Sadness into your life) should be further away, and the people who help you be the best person you can be, should be closer.

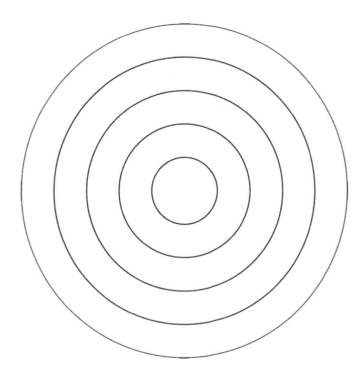

Think about how much personal information you share with people you barely know on social media. What are you going to do differently?

_____
_____
_____
_____
_____
_____
_____
_____

Think about people in your life whose opinion you give too much VALUE to (i.e. Mom, Dad, person you have a crush on, friend, etc.). How are you going to tune them out, so you can focus on what YOU believe is in your best interest?

_____
_____
_____
_____
_____
_____
_____
_____

A good litmus test for a romantic relationship is simply asking yourself, "If today is as good as it gets with (this person), will I be happy?" Have you resolved your own baggage, **or** are you expecting this person to "Make You Happy,"?

_____
_____
_____
_____
_____
_____
_____
_____

If you haven't dealt with/resolved your own shit, then fucking work through it! You don't know how good life can be with another person if you're part of the problem. If you have dealt with/resolved your own shit, then look at your partner. Have they dealt with/resolved their own shit, or are they expecting you to "Make Them Happy,"?

_____
_____
_____
_____
_____
_____
_____
_____

If they haven't dealt with their own shit, do they understand happiness like you do? Are they willing to start working through the frustration, anger, disappointment, and sadness that keeps them from being happy?

___

If you are debating on ending your relationship, figure out where the line in the sand is for you. Is this person causing you frustration, anger, disappointment, and sadness? Is this person working to resolve their own issues and baggage? Is there a genuine connection between you, or were you both looking for a distraction rather than for someone to bring out the best in you?

___

NOTES

CHAPTER 9

ACHIEVING SUCCESS

It's real fucking frustrating to be busting your ass and to see other people achieve success with what seems like absolutely no effort. Everybody has that one "lucky," asshole friend/acquaintance who wins thousands of dollars on scratch-off lotto tickets. What people don't think about is how that same asshole spends thousands of dollars on lotto tickets and only talks about the money he/she won... and never about the money they have lost. Stop looking at "Luck," as being legitimate! Most people who say they just "Got lucky," are generally lying, or they are too humble to tell you the honest truth: they had a better idea than everyone else, they executed an idea better than everyone else, or they simply tried a lot fucking harder than everyone else... Luck had **NOTHING** to do with it.

The latest phone app didn't simply appear out of nowhere- someone had the idea, people had to write the code, and then it had to be promoted to the point where it caught on. The latest YouTube sensation didn't just get big with one video- they had to create hundreds of videos to make a catalog of content. Yet, as consumers, we see the end result and irrationally think that it was "easy," for that person. Think about that YouTube star for 2 seconds... If it were really "easy," why isn't everybody doing it? A lot of people do try- and most of them fail to capture an audience. It's not easy.

Achieving success isn't going to be easy- so get that idea out of your head. Start looking at success like a Mixed Martial Arts (MMA) fight. If you are going to be the champion, you must be the best. In order to be the best, you've got to put in the fucking time, effort, sweat, and dedication. Success follows the same formula regardless of what avenue you are pursuing; from being a professional bodybuilder, to making the best micro-brew, to creating a cure for cancer- the formula to success is always the same: **TIME + CONSISTENCY + DEDICATION/DETERMINATION = SUCCESS.**

There's no way to get around that formula. New Navy Seals graduate from the academy every year; yet, there are many who wash out of the program too. Why? Because it's FUCKING HARD- even for people who were already in great physical shape going into it! Bitching and fixating on the pain and difficulty will not get someone through the training program. Time, Consistency, and Dedication, however, will. You want that promotion? **TIME + CONSISTENCY + DEDICATION/DETERMINATION**. You want to start a successful business? **TIME + CONSISTENCY + DEDICATION/DETERMINATION**. You want to get rich? **TIME + CONSISTENCY + DEDICATION/DETERMINATION**. It's really that fucking simple- it's just not easy…

LESSONS ABOUT SUCCESS

LESSON 1: SUCCESS IS NOT A RACE, SO WHERE YOU START DOESN'T MATTER!

So many people have a preconceived idea that if you grow-up beat, broken, and poor, you'll never succeed. It doesn't matter how many Oprah Winfrey stories there are, society casts those stories as the "exception," instead of the rule.

Why are these stories ALWAYS being made out to be the exception? Because there is misplaced **PITY** for those who don't succeed. That sounds harsh as fuck, until you really break it down. A kid from a wealthy family grows up with a safety net that prevents him/her from building motivation and determination. For many wealthy kids, success is an option, not a requirement, because Mommy and Daddy will pick them up if or when they fall. Now consider a poor kid. They have no safety net to save them if they only make a half-assed effort. Wealthy kids know what success looks like, feels like, and tastes like. However, they don't know and understand **STRUGGLE**. Poor kids know **STRUGGLE**, but haven't experienced what success looks, feels, and tastes like. Now, which one is going to be more willing to grind through the hard times to reach success?

Even beyond looking at "Rich vs. Poor," people fuck things up by thinking that "SUCCESS," is some type of race. Dig this...

THERE IS NO FINSIH LINE! Think about that point for a good long minute. Even if everyone was to "Start," at the exact same point, there is no defined "Finish Line," other than DEATH. One person might determine "Success," to be making $50 thousand a year at a steady job. Someone else might define success as being a boss who makes $100+ thousand per year. Another person might define success as being the owner of a company that makes $1 million per year. Are any of them wrong? No- everyone has their own idea of what it means to be "Successful."

Since there is no "Finish Line," does it matter where you start? Fuck no! Take it a step further: who the hell are you trying to race against? Are you any less successful if you become a millionaire at age 30, even though a high-school kid gets a multimillion-dollar NBA contract when he's 19-years-old? No. Is gramps less of a success because he cracks $20 million at age 72, even though you hit $20 million at 42? No. Why? Because you're not fucking racing anyone!

Stop having a pity-party for yourself or allowing other people to throw them in your honor! It doesn't matter where you start. Do you want it? Do you want it even though you've never seen it, felt it, or tasted it? Do you still want it even though you're going to struggle and won't be able to achieve it with a half-assed effort? Do you still want it even if takes you longer than someone else? That's what the shit all boils down to: "**HOW FUCKING BAD DO YOU WANT TO BE SUCCESSFUL?" TIME + CONSISTENCY + DEDICATION/DETERMINATION = SUCCESS.**
Expecting more for less is dumb, and giving anything less than what is needed, is just an excuse.

LESSON 2: EQUAL OPPORTUNITY DOESN'T MEAN EQUAL SUCCESS

Too many fucking people get butt-hurt because they saw someone succeed, but when they tried, they failed. Guess what? That's life! You didn't walk in their shoes! You have no clue if they failed a million times before you saw them "make it." Unless you were with them every step of the way, you don't honestly know how hard they were trying. They might have failed once, twice, or a million fucking times, but you only saw the success. You can't compare your failure against other people's success.

Moreover, you have to dig real fucking deep and ask yourself how bad do you really want it?! Is one failure going to stop you? Is two failures going to stop you? If you want to succeed bad enough, you will get back up- **EACH AND EVERY FUCKING TIME** and then try again- but a little bit harder next time. You learned to walk, because you were willing to fall. You learned to ride a bike, because you were willing to crash. You learned to read, write, count, and do countless other things because you were willing to fail. You want to succeed? Be willing to fall, crash, and fail again and again. It might take you more failures than 10 other people, but **IT DOESN'T FUCKING MATTER!** The only thing that matters is that **YOU ARE WILLING TO FAIL UNTIL YOU ARE SUCCESSFUL!**

LESSON 3: STOP CARING ABOUT WHAT OTHER PEOPLE THINK

You got an idea for free energy? People will tell you that you are crazy (just look up Nikola Tesla).   Think you have what it takes to be an actor or artist? People will tell you that you are dreaming. Think you want to be an entrepreneur and start your own company? People will remind you where you came from.

Mom, Dad, Granny- they might tell you this shit because they are fucking **SCARED FOR YOU**. They love you, and don't want to see you get hurt. However, getting hurt is part of the game. Remember those scrapes you got when you were learning to ride a bike? It's going to happen.

There are other people who care about you, but they don't want you to leave. These are generally your friends. As much as they want you to succeed, they know that if you get out, you ain't coming back! They are thinking that if you're gone, they'll be all alone. They're thinking about how "Unfair," it would be that you come from the same area/background and will be living "Miller's High-Life," while they will just be the low-life left behind. Remember High School? Think about the friends you had when you were there, and how quickly the dynamic changed after graduation (or you dropped out). Some people started working. Some people went to college. Other people joined the military. When High School was over, your "crew," wasn't the same. Subconsciously, people remember that. This is why your friends fear that your success will be the end of your friendship.

The last group of people are just acquaintances. These people are fucking miserable and would shit on you even if you DID find the cure for cancer. You'll never be good enough to them, because IF they acknowledged your success, then they would have to acknowledge how they don't measure up to you. The best way for them to tower over you, is to chop you down at your knees.

Regardless of their reasoning, you have to stop caring and worrying about what other people think. This is your life. These are your goals, ambitions, and dreams. You have to **DECIDE WHAT YOU WANT**, and remind yourself why it's important. Otherwise, everyone will hold you back.

The other side of this ordeal, is worrying about your own prestige. People get really wrapped up in the idea of glitz, glamour, and fame, and think that if they do not have it, then they are not successful. It's a really fucked up mindset because glitz, glamour, and fame do not equate to success for MOST entrepreneurs.

If you start your own company that cleans up dog shit in people's yards- guess what? You're an entrepreneur! Are you going to be famous? No! If you start your own engineering firm, making plastic cases for smartphones, you're an entrepreneur. Are you going to be famous? No! If you start your own shampoo, fragrance, or make-up line- you're an entrepreneur. Are you going to be famous? Not likely!

Dig this- just because you're an entrepreneur doesn't mean you're going to be famous. Jeff Bezos is one of the richest men in the world because he owns most of the shares of the company he started, Amazon. But you wouldn't be likely to recognize him if he passed you in a crowd. Warren Buffet was once the richest man in the world, but you would dismiss him if you saw him in person, because you wouldn't immediately recognize him. If you want attention and fame, then you better seek a career in the spotlight- actor/actress, or a singer.

LESSON 4: FOOLS CHASE MONEY, SUCCESSFUL PEOPLE CHASE THEIR DREAMS

The problem with chasing money is that **SUCCESS = TIME + CONSISTENCY + DEDICATION/DETERMINATION.** So, unless you are always insanely fixated on the next "Money move," you are most likely to burn out before you make the big money you desire. This is also the reason why so many businesses fail. Too many businesses fixate on maximizing profits, rather than providing the best goods/services to their customers. Look at the companies and businesses that rode their profits into bankruptcy: Sears (started off as a catalog company... killed off by Amazon- which is nothing but an "On-line," catalog company), Blockbuster Video (Killed off by Netflix and Redbox), or Palm (they made "PDA's" or personal digital assistants, which were essentially the first iPhones of the 1990's and early 2000's- now dead because of Apple).

When the money doesn't immediately start rolling in (or in some cases, slows down) people tend to lose focus on the essential formula for success: **TIME + CONSISTENCY + DEDICATION/DETERMINATION**. It's really easy to get lazy, lose focus, or even give up when your "heart isn't into it." On the flip side, when your heart is deeply vested into something, it's much easier to weather the storms and the hard times.

Take Nike for example. Nike was started by Phil Knight and his high school track coach Bill Bowerman. Nike didn't start off as a glamorous multi-billion-dollar organization. Its humble origins started with Bowerman and Knight selling their shoes out of the trunks of their cars. However, since they were passionate about it, the company outgrew anyone's expectations 20 years later. How did they do it? **TIME + CONSISTENCY + DEDICATION/DETERMINATION**. Nike wasn't an "overnight success,"; instead, it remained focused and persistent over 20 years, and **grew** into the athletic wear empire that we know it as today.

It's insanely hard to invest **TIME + CONSISTENCY + DEDICATION/DETERMINATION** if your heart isn't into it. That is why it is often easier/better to chase your dreams, than it is to just chase the next thing that will make money.

LESSON 5: WRITE IT OUT

A builder starts with blueprints. Most people casually think about blueprints as if they are just as a generalized idea of how some shit is going to look when it's done. Nothing could be further from the truth. Those blueprints have stages. This first stage is the foundation. The next stage is the support beams and structure. The next step is roofing, doors, and windows. The next stage is electrical, plumbing, heating, and cooling. The next stage is outside finishing (insulation, siding, etc). The last stage is inside finishing (drywall, paint, decoration). Each of those stages have a complete rundown of measurements/dimensions, materials, and specific details of how everything is going to be installed/assembled (like stud/beam placement, how wiring/plumbing will be routed, etc.).

Why is that important? Because shit's going to be pretty fucked up if you don't **KNOW EXACTLY** what the end result is supposed to be. Beyond that, imagine what happens if people are doing random shit out of order- like finishing interior drywall if there is no roof, exterior walls, or windows to protect it from the rain/sleet/snow. Imagine running plumbing and electrical wires across spaces where there is supposed to be windows or a doorway. This is why blueprints are made.

SUCCESS = TIME + CONSISTENCY + DEDICATION/DETERMINATION. People often fail to become successful because they waste time and resources doing shit out of order- like ordering 10,000 custom shirts, before they've ever tried to even sell 10 on their own, or leasing office space, before they've figured out why they even need an office outside of their home.

Successful people make "blueprints," for their success. They know what stages they will have to go through. They know what work must be done at each stage. They know what the end result is going to be. This way their time is used proficiently, and their efforts aren't wasted because shit is done out of order.

You can simplify this "blueprinting" with the "ACE" method. When planning out your success, first figure out what the stages will be, then map out each stage. Think about building your success, just like you would build a skyscraper- little details can be the difference between achievement and disaster.

Break it down. What **Action** are you trying to achieve (i.e. starting your own business)? List out the **Commitment** that it is going to take in order to make this Action happen: steps, time, resources, and effort. Detail what the **End Result** is going to look like (Be as specific as possible). Continuously refine **Action** and **Commitment** to ensure that they align with the **End Result** you desire.

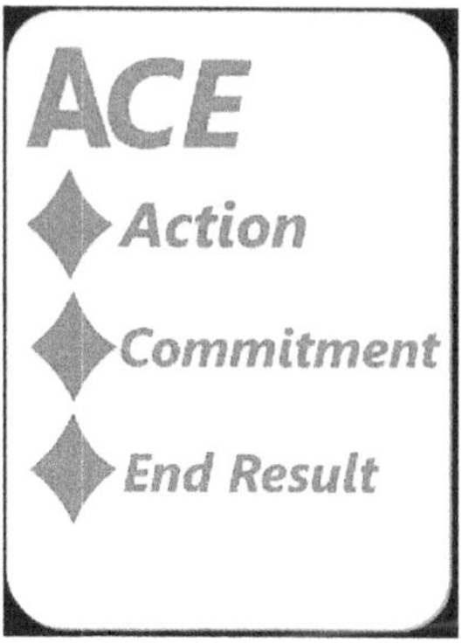
ACE
Action
Commitment
End Result

LESSON 6: LEARN FROM YOUR MISTAKES

Would you play a video game if it were stuck on "super easy," mode? Fuck no! It would be too dull and boring. Life is a series of adventures. Each stage has its own unique challenges. You will have to learn how to overcome the next puzzle, the next problem, and the next failure. The world isn't against you, it just doesn't fucking care. You succeed, or you fail, life will go on. You live, or you die, the world around you will go on. Don't take the shit personally- because it's not personal. The world just doesn't fucking care. This is your movie or your RPG video game, learn from your mistakes and conquer the level so you can move onto the next. Train yourself to embrace the challenges in the world, rather than fixating on how much you wish they were different.

LESSON 7: DON'T LOOK FOR PARTNERS IF YOU CAN DO IT ALONE

This gets people into a lot of confrontations. People often have an idea, and then try to start a business with a family member, friend, or team of people. Shit hits the fan because the person with the idea generally starts to think they are the "boss," and everyone else should do the work, or that they are entitled to extra benefits (Because, it was "Their idea,"). If other people sign paperwork as "partners," not as "employees," there's going to be some fucking problems. The flip side of the coin, is the person with the idea may end up working 10x harder than their "partners," because the business is their "baby," while the partners view the business simply as a prospect to make money.

Partners are great if everyone is equally vested with their **TIME + CONSISTENCY + DEDICATION/ DETERMINATION.** However, that is rarely the case, and most often, shit falls apart. Partners mean that you must compromise your ideas. Partners mean that you are equally liable for success. Partners also mean that someone else can get paid while you are doing all of the work.

Assess your ideas and truly think about whether you need to have "partners," or "employees." If you need partners, evaluate them to ensure that they are equally dedicated for the right reason (Passion, not instant profits); otherwise, you too can be Steve Jobs and get tossed from your own company.

LESSON 8: GREED IS THE ROOT OF ALL EVIL

From the time you could talk, you've been told that **MONEY** is the root of all evil- it's not. **GREED** is the root of all evil. Money is paper, precious metals, or now just a digital construct based on an algorithm. Having a lot of money isn't evil. Being willing to hurt other people to get money is- but that happens every day for amounts far less than $100. The money wasn't evil, the greedy asshole willing to do anything imaginable to take it is evil.

In the pursuit of success, you must keep your own greed in check. Don't walk on people as you are building your dreams. Don't take people for granted when things finally start to work out. Don't forget to thank people for their support along the way. Your success is going to be much more fulfilling if you are **GRATEFUL,** and not **GREEDY**.

LESSON 9: STOP MAKING FUCKING EXCUSES

People often fuck themselves by trying to pin the blame for anything and everything on other people and situations. It's his fault, her fault, their fault, it's because of this, it's because of that… anybody but their own-self. Guess what? It is **YOUR FAULT THAT YOU ARE NOT SUCCESSFUL**. You are either too content making excuses, or too fucking laxed in your efforts.

That's a tough pill to swallow, but it's true. Society has become fucking soft, but nobody wants to hear it. Unfortunately, people have been sheltered from the truth for so long, now they are offended by it.

Today, people willingly reject the truth and just want to believe the bullshit. Mom told you it was your teacher's fault that you failed- but you know that you were playing video games instead of studying. Your friends told you that your boss had it out for you- but you know you were fucking off at work and showing up late. Society says that you're not successful because you grew up in poverty and had a rough childhood- but you knew right from wrong, had access to the internet, and had the ability to learn how to do anything from pass a mechanic's exam to registering your own business.

Instead of being truthful with each-other, much less, our own-selves, we sugarcoat the hell out of stupid mistakes. Mothers want to support their children and don't want to believe that their kid is doing dumb shit. Your friends either don't know your work habits or don't want to give you more shit after you get fired. Society doesn't want to shit on you when you had a rough start. Instead of everyone being **HONEST** with you, everyone tries to "be nice," to you with hopes that you will quietly own your fucking mistakes and quit repeating them.

Unfortunately, because society tries to "Be nice," people continue to make stupid mistakes. Moreover, people began losing their damn minds, and started believing the bullshit like it was the gospel! "Yeah Mom, that teacher just had it out for me." "Yeah, my boss was an asshole and just had it out for me." "Yeah, I grew up in the street, and they just have it out for me." Are you fucking kidding me? **STOP IT!**

Steve Harvey had a stuttering problem as a child, lived out of his car for 3 years, fished for his dinner from other people's ponds, and became a multi-millionaire. How? Because he kept trying (**SUCCESS = TIME + CONSISTENCY + DEDICATION/ DETERMINATION**). Why did he keep trying? Because he didn't make excuses to fail, or buy into the bullshit excuses people made for him.

You don't have to be "Book smart," in order to be successful. However, you must have the emotional intelligence to know when you are just lying to yourself. **IT'S OKAY TO ADMIT TO YOURSELF THAT YOU ARE WRONG or THAT YOU FUCKED UP!** It's dumb to make excuses when you know the truth- and lying about it isn't going to change the outcome. Beyond that, if you don't learn from your mistakes, you're setting yourself up to fail again, in the exact same fucking way. Own your shit.

YOU ARE NOT HOPELESS. If you are not actively putting in the **TIME + CONSISTENCY + DEDICATION/ DETERMINATION,** then it's your own damn fault that you are not living the life that you want to have. The biggest roadblock you have… is yourself.

LESSON 10: YOU HAVE ALL OF THE TIME YOU NEED IF YOU START TODAY

People always blame time… "If I only had more time." "Other people have more time to do extra shit." You have all the fucking time that you need to be successful, but you are probably wasting most of it doing dumb shit like getting into arguments on Facebook, trying to impress people on Instagram, binge-watching a TV series on Netflix, playing video games on X-Box, or just sleeping it all away. Be mindful of the fucking distractions in your life.

The easiest way to handle the distractions, is to make your own rules! Want to get physically fit? You can only watch Netflix or Hulu while on a treadmill. Want to learn a second language? Download Rosetta Stone and you must get through a complete lesson before you allow yourself to open the Facebook app. Want to become an entrepreneur? Turn off the video game until you have taken a full page of notes while doing research. **SUCCESS = TIME + CONSISTENCY + DEDICATION/ DETERMINATION.** It's your life; your rules are either going to align you with success or they are going to detour you from it.

WORK THROUGH YOUR SHIT

Decide what you want (legacy/fame/fortune/etc.):

_____
_____
_____
_____
_____
_____
_____
_____

Where you start does not determine where you will end, however, it can serve as motivation. What aspects of your current situation motivates you to seek this success?

_____
_____
_____
_____
_____
_____
_____
_____

Are you simply trying to impress other people? If not, how is your **heart** vested in what you want to achieve?

_____
_____
_____
_____
_____
_____
_____
_____

Start thinking about the "blueprints," for your own success. Thinking in terms of ACE's (Action, Commitment, End Result), what are the main stages going to look like and require you to do/achieve?

_____
_____
_____
_____
_____
_____
_____
_____
_____
_____
_____
_____
_____
_____

How are you going to handle mistakes and failures?

_____
_____
_____
_____
_____
_____
_____
_____

What are you going to do, in order to "Dig in," instead of giving up?

_____
_____
_____
_____
_____
_____
_____
_____

NOTES

CHAPTER 10
LEADERSHIP

This is the last chapter of the book, but this isn't just "Fluff," or "Filler." This chapter is just as important as any other chapter. Why? Because "Leadership," is missing in today's world. Moreover, those who are able to master the skills of real Leadership, will ultimately live more fulfilling lives.

Leadership has been fucking dying since the turn of the century. Unfortunately, this seems to be a regular cycle in the history of mankind. We go from being a world filled with "Leaders," to a world filled with bosses (Authority). The irony is how today's bosses think of themselves as "Leaders," because of their title of authority (i.e. supervisor, manager, executive, president, etc.). Yet, the reality is authority has no direct correlation to leadership.

At first that sounds counterintuitive, until you think about it. A captain in the Navy can order his sailors to jump off the side of the ship because he has the "Authority," to do so. Now, if the ship isn't in immediate danger (i.e. sinking), that would make him a pretty shitty leader. Make sense? Just because someone has a title or rank of authority, does not mean they were instantly endowed with leadership skills. Leadership, like everything else in life, must be learned. This is why the best "leader," may actually be lower ranking member in an organization.

What the fuck happened to leaders- right? How does this cycle happen when the value of real leadership is widely known? There are two main reasons: 1) Superiors promote sycophantic (Ass-kissing) "Yes!" men/women who will do as they are told regardless of its merit, and 2) People become fixated on being **SIGNIFICANT**- even if it is only by title or rank. When these two trends become the social norm, "Authority," will overshadow leadership.

We know from a long-storied history, that if you tell a lie enough times, it becomes accepted as "truth," (like Christopher Columbus being credited for discovering the Americas). Now, we see this same problem in the realm of "Leadership." Social media has intoxicated people with the idea of being **SIGNIFICANT** as if it guarantees prestige. This is prominently seen today in "Virtue Signaling." Yet, the concept is very old, as previous generations saw this with people known as "Bible Thumpers."

The format is always the same, people publicly proclaim their superior morality, but then do things that are directly counter to the "superior morality," that they claim to have (look up televangelist Jim Bakker).

Social media is just the latest avenue for people to be conditioned to accept "Leadership," and "Authority," to mean the same thing. As you know, however, the two are mutually exclusive constructs.

Everyone wants to be significant and to feel **IMPORTANT**. Yet, most people aren't willing to put in the effort to be a great **LEADER** because it's too fucking hard! The most common case-in-point: your parents. Think back through your youth. Did they ever tell you not to do something, even though they did it (i.e. drink alcohol, smoke, or curse)? How did that make you feel as their subordinate? This brings us to the first point of a great leader and why it's hard to be one:

GREAT LEADERS MODEL DESIRED BEHAVIORS FOR OTHERS TO FOLLOW

So fucking simple, yet for many, so hard to do. Have you ever had a boss call you out for cutting out of work early, when they regularly show up late, take extended lunches, and leave early too? Shitty ain't it? It's okay for him/her to do it because they are "The Boss," (the authoritarian), but if you do it… they drag your ass over the coals. Again, this shows how someone who has "Authority," isn't endowed with "Leadership."

If you are a real leader, you will model the behavior you want others to follow- even when you don't think anyone is looking (we live in a world of digital cameras… someone's always looking). This is as simple as: picking up the piece of trash that 20 people in front of you willfully ignored as they walked by, as mundane as staying after work another 4 hours so you're not dumping unfair duties onto other people, or as complicated as trying to work with people in the community to develop resources for at-risk youth.

AUTHORITARIANS CRITICIZE WHILE LEADERS TEACH

Have you ever had a coach belittle you for a botched play as if they were a former pro from the NFL/NBA/NHL/MLB/FIFA? Have you ever had a teacher/professor critique your work as if they were a world-renowned expert in the subject matter? Authoritarians, often think that critiquing someone is "Leadership." They're in charge, anything less than what they expect is WRONG! Again, the divide becomes obvious.

Leaders don't need to criticize- because they understand that mistakes provide an opportunity to TEACH. Find the misunderstanding and get on the same page. Criticizing people makes them shut down, rather than turning it up to the next level. This leads into the next fault...

ORDERS BY THREAT OR FORCE ARE BEST RESERVED FOR WAR

Ever have a boss that constantly threatens to fire you, or have you fired? Most people who have worked for these Authoritarians will tell you how the threats didn't make them work harder- it just made them aware of where the base line was so they could work just hard enough to not get fired. Once that base line was established, then many of these people start playing games just to "get even," with the motherfucker threatening them.

Many manufacturing plants have machines with lasers that ensure that no one has a hand or arm within the machine before it punches out steel parts, or fastens a rivet, or welds pieces together (like the safety beam on most automatic garage door openers). Many foremen, line supervisors, skilled tradesmen, and engineers have looked like fools for hours as they tried to fix a machine that a subordinate simply smeared grease over the safety laser.

Threats or force will not garner respect. Leaders understand that, while Authoritarians never learn it. Make your life easier and learn how to talk to people in a manner that leaves them feeling respected, even if you do not agree with them.

LEADERS ARE TRANSPARENT

Have you ever fucked up but tried to play it off as if it wasn't your fault? Has someone over you (like your boss) ever done that to you? Again, it sucks, but it exemplifies how people with authority are not necessarily leaders. Many people today are afraid to be honest when they fuck up because of the ramifications. Authoritarians are afraid to be honest because they fear that it will ruin their credibility!

Think about that for a moment. Authoritarians literally think, "I'm the one in charge... I can't admit that I was wrong to this person." Yet, if they would have admitted to being wrong, they would have more credibility and actually would have earned more respect from their subordinates. Leaders understand that good, bad, or indifferent, it's best to own the shit, because you will never earn people's trust when they know that you are a fucking liar who will cover his/her own ass first.

TREAT OTHERS THE WAY YOU WANT TO BE TREATED
You have heard it a million and one times, and it's referred to as the "Golden Rule," for a reason- because that's what great leaders do. Authoritarians will delegate work that they, themselves, wouldn't do. Authoritarians dissuade people from seeking success beyond what they have accomplished. Authoritarians are self-centered pricks. Being "In charge," has never made someone a real "LEADER." Leaders exemplify the "Golden Rule," because they know how powerful it is.

People like other people, who are like themselves (most Star Wars, Star Trek, and Comic-Con fanboys aren't going to Roadkill Nights on Woodward Ave. to show off their resto-modded '72 Chevelle with a fuel injected LS1 engine). Leaders understand that even though someone may not be like them, they should still treat them how they would want to be treated, because it will garner their respect. **Don't be an asshole, just because you can be.**

WORK THROUGH YOUR SHIT

Think back to a time where your parent/guardian could have been a better LEADER rather than an AUTHORITARIAN. What could they have done differently?

_____
_____
_____
_____
_____
_____
_____
_____

Think back to a time where your boss or previous boss could have been a better LEADER rather than an AUTHORITARIAN. What could they have done differently?

_____
_____
_____
_____
_____
_____
_____
_____

Think back to a time where you could have been a better LEADER rather than an AUTHORITARIAN. What could they have done differently?

___

Determine what is more important to you, significance of being an authoritarian, or the ability of being a great leader:

___

Determine what is more important to you, looking like you are "right," even if you are wrong, or being able to own the fact that you were wrong? Why is that important?

___

NOTES

Hey there,

You either just finished reading the book, or you are just flipping through it to see what it's all about. If you're just flipping through it, read Chapter 3 about Happiness, and you will quickly be able to tell if it's a worthwhile read for you.

If you finished reading the book, know that I am grateful that you gave it a chance. Thank you. I truly hope that I was able to give you some answers that you were looking for and that this book had a positive impact on your life. If it has, please tell others about it so we (you and I) can help other people improve their lives and make the world a little better. If the book hasn't helped you- I'm sorry, but I hope that you keep looking for the answers you need.

I wish you the very best,

Mark Drake

Made in the USA
Columbia, SC
15 March 2021